100
THINGS TO
KNOW ABOUT

HISTORY

Written by
Laura Cowan, Alex Frith,
Minna Lacey and Jerome Martin

Illustrated by
Federico Mariani and Parko Polo

Layout and design by
Freya Harrison, Lenka Hrehova
and Amy Manning

History expert:
Dr. Anne Millard

What is history?

History is a way of finding out about the past. The past can get lost on the way to the present, so historians have to be like detectives, examining any **evidence**, or **source**, to find out what happened.

Evidence

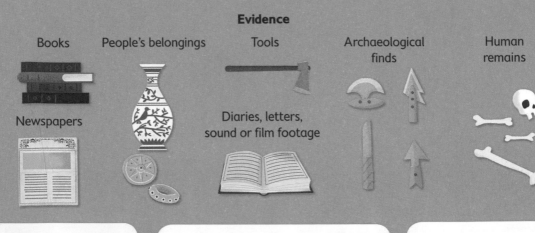

Books

People's belongings

Tools

Archaeological finds

Human remains

Newspapers

Diaries, letters, sound or film footage

Early historians relied on written or spoken sources. Modern historians use anything they can to find out about the past.

Archaeologists, like me, dig up sites and examine what we find — objects, ruins, and even bodies.

The most important rule of history? Never trust a single source to tell the whole story!

History

History isn't just about kings and wars.
Everything has a history, so there are many kinds or **fields**.

All historians ask lots of questions, but we don't always agree on the answers.

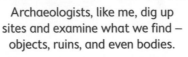

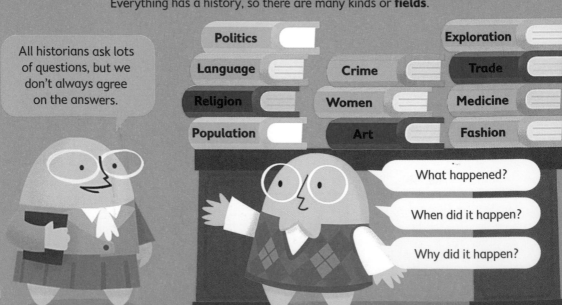

Politics

Exploration

Language

Crime

Trade

Religion

Women

Medicine

Population

Art

Fashion

What happened?

When did it happen?

Why did it happen?

1 History did not begin...

at Year One.

Ancient peoples all had their own ways of recording when things happened. Today, one standard calendar is used around the world, which was devised by early Christian historians. They made the year of Jesus Christ's birth Year One, but a lot of history happened before that.

The present day

AD731
An English monk named Bede wrote *The Ecclesiastical History of the English People*. He was the first writer to use the initials **AD** for the years after the birth of Jesus. This stands for *anno Domini*, which means *in the year of the Lord* in Latin.

The further back you look, the more uncertain dates – as well as everything else – become.

AD525
A Scythian monk, named Dionysius Exiguus, calculated the birth year of Jesus Christ – Year One. Historians today think that Jesus was actually born up to seven years before that.

AD1
Dates before Year One are counted back, starting from **1BC**, which stands for *1 year Before Christ*. There is no year zero.

1BC

4BC

6BC

100BC

3300BC

Today, some people prefer **CE** and **BCE** instead of AD and BC. This stands for *in the Common Era* and *before the Common Era*. Another important letter is **c.** – this stands for the Latin word *circa*, meaning *around*, and goes in front of dates of which historians are unsure.

Some of the first known writing is Sumerian, from c.3000BC.

2 "History" was invented...

by an ancient Greek travel writer.

Over 2,400 years ago, a Greek writer named Herodotus collected and reported eye-witness accounts of battles and other past events, and analyzed their causes and effects. This made him the first true historian.

In 440BC, Herodotus "published" his work by reading it aloud to spectators at the Olympic Games.

And Athens won a stupendous victory over the Persians at the Battle of Marathon...

Herodotus journeyed across Greece and the Mediterranean collecting all kinds of information, including local customs and culture. He called his great works *Histories*. *Historiē* in ancient Greek means *inquiry*.

Herodotus's work tells us a lot about life in ancient times. But not all of his stories are reliable.

For example, he described one-eyed men from northern Europe who fought griffins or dragons for gold.

3 The first paper...
was made from bark, fishing nets and rags.

During the **2nd century**, Cai Lun, an official working for the Chinese emperor, is said to have noticed wasps making papery nests out of chewed-up wood.

Inspired by the wasps, Cai Lun made a paste of pounded mulberry bark, rags and fishing nets. He spread it on a screen and left it to dry...

...and peeled off a sheet of paper.

Over the following centuries, papermaking slowly spread to the rest of the world...

This paper made a far better surface to write on than bamboo, silk or bones, which was what **scribes** – professional writers – had used before.

6th century
Korea and Vietnam

7th century
India and Japan

8th century
Central Asia and the Middle East

11th century
North Africa and Europe

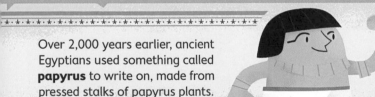

Over 2,000 years earlier, ancient Egyptians used something called **papyrus** to write on, made from pressed stalks of papyrus plants.

Papyrus is not made from pulped wood, so isn't considered to be true paper.

4 New axes were needed...

to settle the New World.

In the 1700s, Europeans began settling along North America's east coast – part of the "New World" as they called it. On arriving, their first priority was to carve out farmland from a landscape of dense, ancient forest. But they soon found their axes just weren't suited to chopping down so many massive trees.

These European axes were based on a pattern that hadn't changed for centuries...

...but, over time, the settlers developed a new, improved design.

Design for European trade axes

- Short, straight handle
- Big, round eye
- Long blade, unstable swing

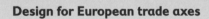

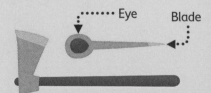
Eye   Blade

Design for American felling axes

- Long, curving handle
- Narrow, triangular eye
- Short blade balanced by a heavy poll
- Can chop down trees *three times faster*

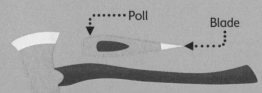
Poll   Blade

This design is still used around the world today.

By the 1850s, Americans were using their new axes to clear an area the size of Manhattan (roughly 60km² or 23 square miles) every 36 hours. This would change the American landscape forever.

A political tool

Axes were such an important part of American culture that, in the 1860s, President Abraham Lincoln included a demonstration of his chopping skills in his public appearances.

5 Making a book took two years...
before printing presses were invented in Europe.

Writing a book can take a long time, but making a new one used to involve copying it out by hand. It was a highly skilled process only carried out by monks for their monasteries or wealthy people.

HOW TO MAKE A BOOK

1 Wash, soak, stretch and scrape animal skin to make parchment.

2 Fold parchment to make 8 pages (a quire) and rule lines ready to write on.

3 Add words by hand using a quill (a sharpened feather) and ink (this is done by a monk, known as a scribe).

4 Paint pictures around the words and add decorated letters, known as illuminations.

5 Sew the book together and bind in leather. Each quire is sewn to cords that make up the spine and pressed down.

Books were very valuable. In Europe, they were only found in the homes of wealthy people, in churches, and in the libraries of monasteries, and, later, universities.

6 Choreomania...
made people dance until they dropped.

Throughout the Middle Ages, people were afflicted by outbreaks of a mysterious dancing plague, or **choreomania**. It struck without warning, was highly contagious, and could be deadly.

One day in 1374, in the streets of the European city of Aachen, someone began dancing – and was unable to stop. Soon, hundreds of others joined in, infected by the dancing plague. They danced wildly, by day and night, stopping only when they collapsed or died from exhaustion.

It was a popular belief that *more* dancing could cure the dancing plague, so people hired professional musicians to accompany the afflicted. The dancers simply staggered on – some groaning in pain, some beset by strange hallucinations. The plague spread gradually to other cities throughout Europe and then, after several weeks, it just petered out.

No one knows what caused the outbreaks of choreomania. At the time, people blamed saints or evil spirits. Today, some historians believe they were caused by a toxic fungus, called ergot, that infected crops. Others think these were cases of mass hysteria, where frightened, superstitious people slipped into a trance-like state.

7 Two US presidents...

were arrested for reckless riding.

Ulysses S. Grant was repeatedly caught speeding in his carriage.

Franklin Pierce was suspected of knocking over a woman with his horse.

This diagram shows the first 40 US presidents, who served from 1789 to 1989.

Reckless riders

Born in Britain

Assassinated

Survived shooting

Avid wrestlers

Kept alligators

Kept parrots

Female

| 1. George Washington | 2. John Adams | 3. Thomas Jefferson | 4. James Madison |

| 5. James Monroe | 6. John Quincy Adams | 7. Andrew Jackson | 8. Martin Van Buren |

| 9. William Henry Harrison | 10. John Tyler | 11. James K. Polk | 12. Zachary Taylor |

| 13. Millard Filmore | 14. Franklin Pierce | 15. James Buchanan | 16. Abraham Lincoln |

Eight of the first nine presidents were born British subjects.

US presidents have one of the most dangerous jobs in the country. **Four** have been assassinated while in office.

Two were shot by would-be assassins, but survived.

Eleven presidents were avid wrestlers.

Abraham Lincoln was a noted champion, winning all but one of about **300** wrestling matches in his lifetime.

Two presidents kept alligators as pets.

Seven presidents kept parrots as pets in the White House.

Andrew Jackson's parrot was known to swear profusely.

| 17. Andrew Johnson | 18. Ulysses S. Grant | 19. Rutherford B. Hayes | 20. James A. Garfield | 21. Chester Arthur | 22. Grover Cleveland |

| 23. Benjamin Harrison | 24. Grover Cleveland | 25. William McKinley | 26. Theodore Roosevelt | 27. William Howard Taft | 28. Woodrow Wilson |

| 29. Warren G. Harding | 30. Calvin Coolidge | 31. Herbert Hoover | 32. Franklin D. Roosevelt | 33. Harry S. Truman | 34. Dwight D. Eisenhower |

| 35. John F. Kennedy | 36. Lyndon B. Johnson | 37. Richard Nixon | 38. Gerald Ford | 39. James Carter | 40. Ronald Reagan |

More than 200 American women have campaigned to become president. **Not one** has been elected.

8 A peasant became Emperor...

and founded one of China's greatest dynasties.

For thousands of years, China was ruled by families, or **dynasties**, that held power for many generations. In 1368, a peasant warrior named Zhu Yuanzhang defeated the **Yuan** dynasty, becoming the first emperor of the new **Ming** dynasty. The Ming achieved many great things.

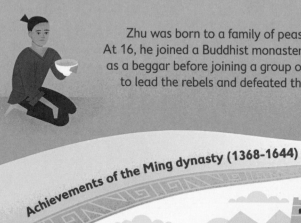

Zhu was born to a family of peasant farmers. At 16, he joined a Buddhist monastery, and later lived as a beggar before joining a group of rebels. He rose to lead the rebels and defeated the Yuan rulers.

Achievements of the Ming dynasty (1368–1644)

Forbidden city
The emperor's vast palace built in Beijing

Great Wall of China
Stretches over 21,000km (13,000 miles) completed during the Ming dynasty

Yongle Encyclopedia
Once the biggest encyclopedia in the world, written by over 2,000 scholars

Ming vases
Made of fine porcelain, which became highly prized throughout the world

Grand Canal
Longest canal in the world, stretches 1,800km (1,100 miles)

9 A pigeon won a medal...

but it cost her a leg.

October 4, 1918
US Major Charles Whittlesey and his battalion of soldiers were trapped in a deep ravine behind enemy lines in France, out of range of radio signals.

They sent three messenger pigeons out of the ravine to get help.

Two were shot dead...

...but a third, Whittlesey's own pet, named Cher Ami, managed to reach US Army Headquarters despite being shot twice.

This meant a rescue mission was able to find and rescue the battalion.

Cher Ami was given the *Croix de Guerre* medal for bravery.

10 Eleven days disappeared...

in September 1752.

People in England going to bed on September 2, 1752 woke up the next day on September 14. This was because the country switched from an old dating system, the **Julian calendar**, to a new one, the **Gregorian calendar**, which brought England in line with most of Europe.

Julian calendar

When: Adopted by Julius Caesar in 45BC
Where: Roman Empire
Timescale: 1 year = 365.25 days. Most years were given 365 days, but an extra day – called a **leap day** – was added every four years.

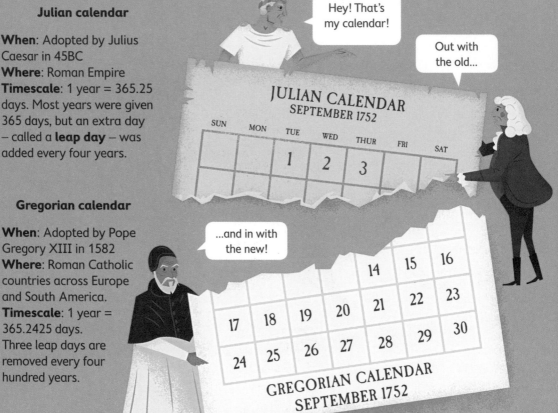

Hey! That's my calendar!

Out with the old...

JULIAN CALENDAR
SEPTEMBER 1752

SUN	MON	TUE	WED	THUR	FRI	SAT
		1	2	3		

Gregorian calendar

When: Adopted by Pope Gregory XIII in 1582
Where: Roman Catholic countries across Europe and South America.
Timescale: 1 year = 365.2425 days. Three leap days are removed every four hundred years.

...and in with the new!

			14	15	16
17	18	19	20	21	22	23
24	25	26	27	28	29	30

GREGORIAN CALENDAR
SEPTEMBER 1752

Scientists define a year as the time it takes for the Earth to orbit around the Sun once.

The Julian calendar was a little slow compared to the speed of Earth's orbit. This meant that the seasons stopped lining up with the right months.

Between 1582 and 1752, England was out of step with much of Europe. The mismatch of dates created some curious anomalies...

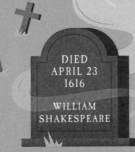

English King William III set sail from Holland on November 11, 1688...

DIED
APRIL 23
1616

MIGUEL
CERVANTES

DIED
APRIL 23
1616

WILLIAM
SHAKESPEARE

Spanish author Miguel Cervantes died ten days before English playwright William Shakespeare — but both deaths have the same date.

...and arrived in Britain later that day, on November 5.

11 Three months disappeared...
from the year 1751 – sort of.

Before switching to the Gregorian calendar, the English government voted to change the date of the New Year. The first day of the year had always been March 25, also known as **Lady Day**, but from 1752, they agreed to start the New Year on January 1.

So, in England and its colonies around the world, the year 1751 ran from March 25 to December 31...

...three months shorter than any year before or since.

YEAR 1751

MARCH	APRIL	MAY	JUNE
JULY	AUGUST	SEPTEMBER	
OCTOBER	NOVEMBER	DECEMBER	

Accountants thought the change was unfair — so the financial year didn't change in the UK. This now begins on April 6, the date that had been March 25 in the Julian calendar.

12 Elephants crossed the Alps...

to attack the Roman army.

Over 2,200 years ago, Hannibal, a general from the city of Carthage in North Africa, astonished his Roman enemies by marching his army, including 40 African war elephants, over the Alps mountains to invade Rome.

The Romans were expecting any attack to come from the south by sea. But instead, Hannibal attacked from the north by land.

Hannibal's surprise attack helped him win a series of battles against the Roman army, and to win control of much of Italy for 15 years.

Rhone river

The Pyrenees

The Alps

Mediterranean Sea

Hannibal set off from New Carthage (now Cartagena), a Carthaginian sea port in southern Spain.

Rome

New Carthage

Carthage

AFRICA

Eventually the Romans fought back by attacking North Africa. Hannibal was forced to retreat to defend his own lands, and was finally defeated in 202BC.

- ⬤ Roman lands
- ⬤ Carthaginian lands
- ⚔ Major battles
- ╴ Hannibal's route
- ━ Roman army's route

13 Dazzle camouflage...
didn't hide ships – but it made them harder to hit.

During the First World War, German submarines sank thousands of enemy vessels. Their sneak attacks were so devastating that the British and American navies resorted to an innovative type of camouflage for their ships.

Known as **dazzle camouflage**, it didn't make ships less visible, but could confuse the captains of attacking submarines.

View through a submarine periscope

Each ship was painted with a unique pattern of contrasting stripes and zig-zags, designed to disrupt the outline of the camouflaged ship.

These patterns made it hard for attackers, peering through a periscope, to judge the ship's size, speed and direction of travel.

I'm not even sure what it IS!

How fast is it going?

Submarine captains aimed torpedoes by sight, so even a slight miscalculation could result in a miss.

14 Vikings spent more time skiing...
than fighting.

The people who lived in Scandinavia (Norway, Sweden and Denmark) around 1,000 years ago are often known as **Vikings**. Although they are noted for fighting and raiding other lands, this usually only took place for a short time during the calendar year.

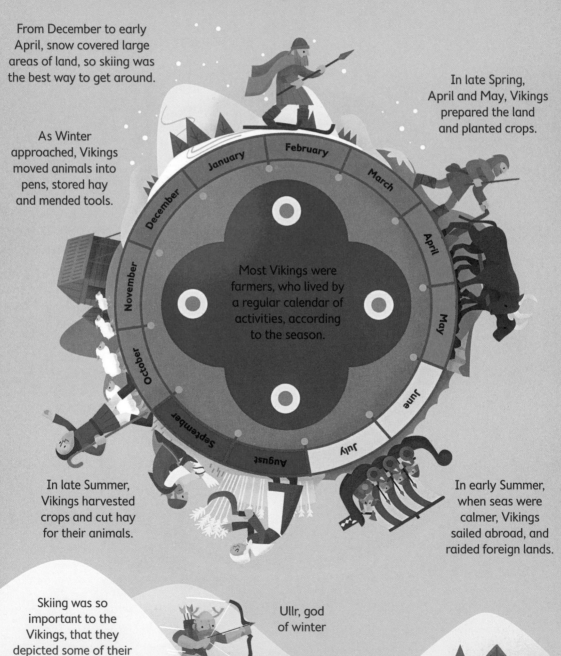

From December to early April, snow covered large areas of land, so skiing was the best way to get around.

As Winter approached, Vikings moved animals into pens, stored hay and mended tools.

In late Spring, April and May, Vikings prepared the land and planted crops.

January
February
March
December
April
November
May
October
June
September
July
August

Most Vikings were farmers, who lived by a regular calendar of activities, according to the season.

In late Summer, Vikings harvested crops and cut hay for their animals.

In early Summer, when seas were calmer, Vikings sailed abroad, and raided foreign lands.

Skiing was so important to the Vikings, that they depicted some of their gods wearing skis.

Ullr, god of winter

15 Eleanor of Aquitaine...

was queen of rival countries that went to war.

Born 1122

1137

At 15, Eleanor, ruler of Aquitaine, married a distant cousin, who became King Louis VII of France.

1147-1149

Alongside Louis, Eleanor led an army on the Second Crusade – an unsuccessful war against the Turks.

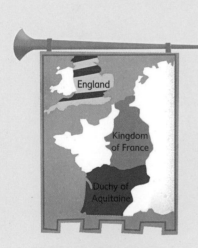

England

Kingdom of France

Duchy of Aquitaine

The marriage brought Aquitaine, which had been part of France, under England's rule. This put both countries on a path to war.

1152

Eleanor divorced Louis, and soon remarried. Her new husband became King Henry II of England in 1154.

1173

Eleanor and three of her sons rebelled against Henry – but failed. Eleanor spent the next 16 years imprisoned, but was freed in 1189 after Henry's death.

1204

Eleanor died at 82. She lived to see her sons, Richard and John, both become kings of England – and a granddaughter (by Louis), become queen of France.

16 Most pyramids...
are in Central America, not Egypt.

Egyptian pyramids are the most famous, but many other cultures have also built pyramid-style structures – often as burial places for rulers or temples to gods.

The Mesopotamians built terraced pyramid-like monuments, known as **ziggurats**, with temples on top.

Modern architects still build pyramids, for instance at the Louvre Art Gallery in Paris, France.

▲ = 10 pyramids

Mesopotamia (Iraq) – **30** pyramids
Sumerian, Babylonian, Assyrian empires   3000BC-500BC

Egypt – about **130** pyramids   2600BC-1600BC

Peru – **250** pyramids
Norte Chico, Moche, Chimu and Inca   2000BC-1532

Nubia and Sudan – **250** pyramids

Kushite Kingdoms   700BC-300

Mexico, Guatemala, Belize, Honduras, El Salvador – **1,000** pyramids
Olmec, Aztec, Maya   1000BC-1697

Egypt's Great Pyramid of Giza was 146.5m (481 feet) high on completion. For 3,800 years, it was the world's tallest structure made by people.

17 Anti-burglar devices...

were fitted in ancient Egyptian tombs.

The tombs of Egyptian pharaohs were filled with such precious treasures that they were built with secret passages, dead ends and blocked entrances – to put off grave robbers.

Pyramid tomb of Pharaoh Amenemhat III who ruled from about 1860-1814BC

Portcullises – huge stone slabs that blocked the passageways

Burial chamber
Heavy stone blocks sealed the burial chamber, where Amenemhat III's body lay in a wooden coffin surrounded by treasure.

This **passageway** led to a dead end. Tomb robbers would have wasted a lot of time looking for a burial chamber along here.

A secret trapdoor in the ceiling led to a hidden passageway to the burial chamber.

······ Stairway

The Egyptians believed that after death, they would go to another world, known as the *Afterlife*. So kings were buried with treasure and goods that they would need there.

Osiris - god of the Afterlife

The **outside entrance** to the tomb was blocked up and would have been impossible to detect after the Pharaoh's funeral.

Despite all these devices, by around 1000BC, all of Egypt's 130 pyramids had been robbed.

18 The world's longest hedge...

grew across the middle of British-ruled India.

From the 1840s to the 1870s, British officials in India were so desperate to prevent smuggling that they set up a customs barrier that crossed almost the whole country. Most of it was grown from local plants, earning the nickname the **Great Hedge of India**.

Total length: 4,030km (2,504 miles)
Max. height: 3.7m (12ft)
Max. thickness: 4.3m (14ft)

Eastern side:
Princely states, a collection of regions ruled by princes, but indirectly controlled by Britain.

Western side:
British India, ruled directly by British politicians

Officials wanted to stop people on the eastern side from smuggling valuable salt to the western side without paying taxes.

SALT

Some stretches of the "hedge" went across wilderness, where plants couldn't grow — but people couldn't cross, either.

The hedge included over 1,700 customs posts, staffed by a total of 12,000 men.

Different sections of the hedge were grown from these plants:

 Indian plum   acacia

 babool   prickly pear

19 Surviving a nuclear explosion...

was just the start for 160 *niju hibakusha.*

In the sixth year of the Second World War, American bombers dropped a nuclear weapon onto the Japanese city of Hiroshima. Some of the survivors of the attack, known in Japanese as *hibakusha*, were hit again, when a second bomb landed on Nagasaki three days later.

Hiroshima
August 6, 1945
Uranium bomb named **Little Boy**
People killed: around **70,000**
People injured: around **76,000**

Nagasaki
August 9, 1945
Plutonium bomb named **Fat Man**
People killed: around **40,000**
People injured: around **21,000**

JAPAN
Honshu
island

Kyushu
island

Double danger

Many people who were injured in the Hiroshima blast made a two-day journey to reach Nagasaki, hoping to recover in peace. Of these, **160** of these survived the second bomb attack. They're recognized as *niju hibakusha*, or *double survivors*.

One of these, an engineer named Yamaguchi Tsumoto, spent a decade recovering from burns. But he went on to live until 2010, aged 93.

These two weapons caused such devastation that Japan surrendered, ending the War.

20 An expedition achieved its aim...

only by vanishing in the polar wastes.

In 1845, two ships sailed from England to the icy waters of northern Canada. Their aim was to find the **Northwest Passage** – an Arctic sea route from the Atlantic to the Pacific – but the ships simply disappeared. It was their would-be rescuers who, years later, fulfilled that objective.

With 129 men and a celebrated leader named Sir John Franklin, this polar expedition was meant to be the largest, best-equipped ever.

When it failed to return, countries around the world sent rescue ships to search for any survivors.

Despite combing the Arctic for decades, the searchers found little more than driftwood, an abandoned boat, some skeletons and hundreds of scattered bones.

A single, scribbled note, discovered in a pile of rocks in 1859, described the expedition's rapid downward spiral.

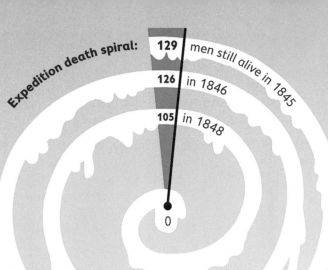

Expedition death spiral:

129 | men still alive in 1845
126 | in 1846
105 | in 1848
0

Franklin's ships had become trapped in thick ice. The crews were slowly dying of hunger, a condition called scurvy, and other ailments — including severe lead poisoning from the ships' water tanks.

Eventually, those left alive tried to walk hundreds of miles south to safety, dragging their dwindling supplies across the ice in boats and on sleds.

None survived the journey.

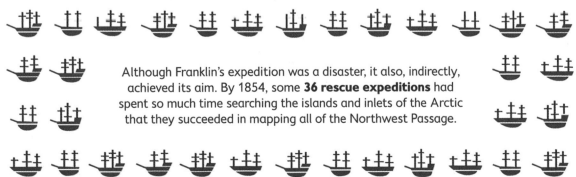

Although Franklin's expedition was a disaster, it also, indirectly, achieved its aim. By 1854, some **36 rescue expeditions** had spent so much time searching the islands and inlets of the Arctic that they succeeded in mapping all of the Northwest Passage.

21 A pacifist with no clothes...
started life as a prince.

Mahavira was born a prince in India around 2,600 years ago. He left home at age 30 and devoted his years to discovering the secret of living a perfect life – a secret he soon shared, known today as the religion **Jainism**.

Two of Mahavira's central teachings were **aparigraha** and **ahimsa**.

Aparigraha means not owning any possessions, including clothes.

Ahimsa means not doing harm to any person, animal – or even an insect.

Choosing to give up a normal life, and taking on hardships such as fasting, is called **asceticism**. Ascetic practices have existed in nearly all religions.

Stylites
(Orthodox Christianity)
spend years at a time praying on top of pillars, relying on passers-by for food.

Dervishes
(Sufi Islam)
beg for money so they can give it away to people in need.

Nichiren monks
(Mahayana Buddhism)
spend the winter undergoing three-hourly purifying rituals under an ice-cold waterfall.

22 A symbol of happiness...
became a symbol of hatred.

A symbol called a **swastika** has been used by cultures all around the world since ancient times. The first people known to use it lived in the Indus Valley, mainly in what is now Pakistan, around 5,000 years ago.

The symbol was first named by Hindus writing in Sanskrit. *Swastika* roughly translates as "wellbeing" or "good luck".

In time, Jains and Buddhists adopted the symbol too, to denote goodness and happiness.

Navajo people in North America have long used the symbol to represent good health. They call it 'the whirling log'.

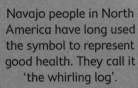

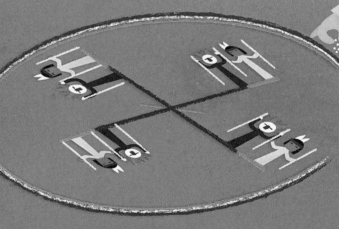

In certain ceremonies, Navajo healers paint the whirling log pattern on the ground using powdered minerals, sand, corn meal and pollen.

In the 1920s in Germany, a political party called the National Socialists, or **Nazis**, put a swastika on its flag. The design was chosen by the party's leader, Adolf Hitler.

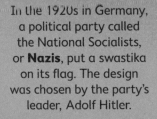

For Hitler, the swastika was a link to the ancient Indo-Europeans he believed were the ancestors of the Germans. He soon started the Second World War, and ordered the murder of millions of people, especially Jews and Roma. Ever since, people have associated swastikas with hate.

23 Peter really was *Great*...
and Ivan really was *Terrible*.

	Peter the Great	Isabel the Redeemer	Alfonso the Troubadour

7
6
5
4
3
2
1

Tsar of Russia
Reigned: 1682–1721
Height: 203cm (6ft, 8in)
– almost a head taller
than most people.

Princess Imperial of Brazil
Reigned: 1850–1891
Campaigned for and signed
off the Golden Law, which
freed all slaves in Brazil.

King of Aragon
Reigned: 1164–1196
Composed and
performed his
own poetry.

24 Alexander the Great...
named a city after his horse.

His horse was one of many celebrity horses that appear in history books.

Bucephalus (c.355–326BC)
A fierce battle horse who would only
consent to be ridden by Alexander the
Great. When he died, the Macedonian
conqueror named a city after him.

Incitatus (1st century)
As the Roman emperor Caligula's horse,
he dined on oats mixed with gold flakes.
It's said that Caligula considered making
him a senator, as an insult to senators.

Ivan the Terrible

Coloman the Bookish

Wladyslaw the Elbow

Tsar of Russia
Reigned: 1547-1584
Prone to fits of terrible,
murderous rage, including once
when he killed his own son.

King of Hungary
Reigned: 1095-1116
Known across Europe for
being extremely intelligent
and well-read.

King of Poland
Reigned: 1320-1333
Elbow meant *elbow-high* –
although there is no record
of his precise height.

Marocco (c.1586-c.1606)
A performing horse who toured Europe,
he could walk on two legs, play dead, and
count coins. Due to his uncanny abilities,
his trainer was twice accused of sorcery.

Huaso (1933-1961)
After a mediocre racing career, this Chilean
horse was retrained to be a high-jumper.
Seventy years later, no other horse has ever
jumped higher than his record 2.47m (8ft 1in).

25 Killer exams...

could be the death of students in China.

From the 7th to the 19th centuries, almost anyone in China could become a government official. This meant great influence and status – but only if they passed a set of demanding tests known as the **Imperial Examinations**.

1 **Basic level tests:** *shengyuan* (pass rate 10-20%)

Calligraphy

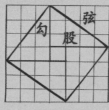

Mathematics

Law, based on the works of philosopher Confucius

Horse riding and archery

After many years of study, successful *shengyuan* candidates tried their luck at the top level:

2 **Top level tests:** *jinshi* (pass rate 1-2%)

- Demonstrate a style of writing known as an "eight-legged essay"

- Compose original poetry

From the 14th century, the *jinshi* tests lasted for **three days and two nights**.

Candidates sat side by side in tiny cubicles. They had to provide their own paper and ink.

Some couldn't cope with the pressure, and were too nervous to eat or sleep.

Rule books outlined procedures for dealing with candidates who died while taking the exams.

26 Roman slaves and their owners...

switched roles once a year.

The usual rules of society were abandoned every year during an ancient Roman festival called *Saturnalia*. Gifts were exchanged, and there was wild feasting, with masters serving food and drink to their slaves.

Crowns of leaves were worn by men and women.

Everyone dance!

Masters dressed as slaves or commoners, for example wearing a felt hat called a *pilleus*.

One person, often a slave, was chosen to be the Roman god Saturn. He was the "King of Misrule" in charge of festivities.

Saturnalia inspired similar festivals in many other countries, hundreds of years later.

Medieval England
Twelfth Night
(January 5)
A chosen "Lord of Misrule" could give silly tasks to both nobles and peasants.

Medieval France
Feast of Fools
(January 1)
Some churchmen swapped roles, dressed up as women or wore masks.

27 Iron from space...

was used for hunting Arctic seals.

For hundreds of years, people living in the Arctic made weapons and tools using iron harvested from meteorites.

There are few usable sources of iron in the frozen landscapes north of the Arctic Circle. So, from about the 8th century, local people relied on iron-rich meteorites that fell from the sky.

The most famous of these is the **Cape York Meteorite**, which landed in Greenland about 10,000 years ago.

It broke into huge pieces, one of them weighing around **31 tons**. People came from far away to hammer chunks of iron from it.

These chunks of iron were shaped into knives, arrowheads, harpoon blades and other tools that were traded all across the Arctic.

28 The Flute of Shame...

was a punishment for bad musicians.

Punishments were a lot more cruel and inventive in the past. The Flute of Shame was used to punish bad musicians in medieval Amsterdam.

The flute was hung from the neck by an iron collar and the musician's fingers were clamped on here.

Medieval Amsterdam

16th-century Germany

There were many different shame masks that people had to wear in public as punishment for behaving badly. This mask was for 'behaving like a pig'.

19th-century Britain

D

If schoolchildren got something wrong, they had to stand in the corner of a classroom wearing a dunce's cap made of paper.

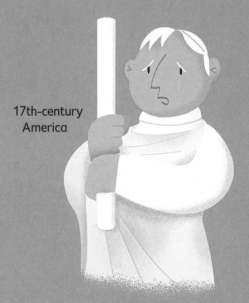

17th-century America

The punishment for disrespecting church officials was standing in church every Sunday in a white sheet, holding a white wand.

29 The cat o'nine tails...

kept order on board ships.

For hundreds of years, naval captains believed the best way to keep their crews safe at sea was to use punishments for almost any crime, big or small. One of the most common was a series of lashes from a nine-tassled whip known as the **cat o'nine tails.**

Here are some of the crimes that earned the cat, based on an 18th-century rule book from the British Royal Navy:

Punishments were always given on deck, where the crew was forced to watch.

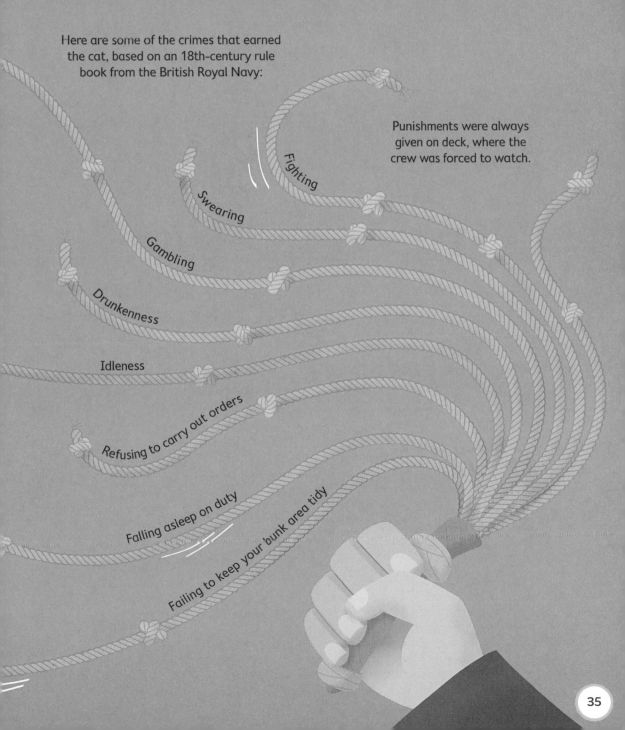

Fighting

Swearing

Gambling

Drunkenness

Idleness

Refusing to carry out orders

Falling asleep on duty

Failing to keep your bunk area tidy

30 A game of cricket...

was the first ever sports match between two nations.

On September 24, 1844, St. George's cricket club in Manhattan hosted a two-day match between the USA and Canada. This match is the oldest recorded sporting fixture played by teams representing rival countries.

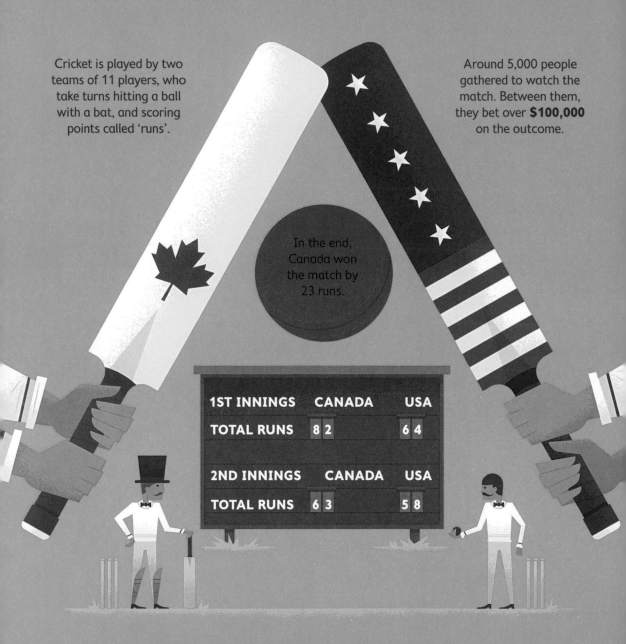

Cricket is played by two teams of 11 players, who take turns hitting a ball with a bat, and scoring points called 'runs'.

Around 5,000 people gathered to watch the match. Between them, they bet over **$100,000** on the outcome.

In the end, Canada won the match by 23 runs.

1ST INNINGS	CANADA	USA
TOTAL RUNS	8 2	6 4

2ND INNINGS	CANADA	USA
TOTAL RUNS	6 3	5 8

Cricket is no longer widely played in Canada or the US. During the late 19th century, a new game that was faster and required less equipment became far more popular – baseball.

31 One of the first female doctors...

was named James.

Margaret Ann Bulkley was the first person born female to go to medical school in Britain, in 1809. At that time only men were allowed to study medicine, so Margaret Ann became James. Throughout history, others have overcome similar challenges.

Who do I want to be...?

Alonso Díaz Ramírez de Guzmán aka **Catalina de Erauso** (1592–1650)

Soldier in Spanish Army

Alexander Sokolov aka **Nadezdha Durova** (1783-1866)

Soldier in Polish Horse Regiment

British military surgeon

Dr. James Barry aka **Margaret Ann Bulkley** (c.1789-1865)

Chinese warrior

Hua Mulan (5th or 6th century)

American stagecoach driver and rancher

One-Eyed Charley Parkhurst aka **Charlotte Parkhurst (**1812-1879)

Some of these people kept their secret until their deaths.

The latest dark age...

has only just begun.

Historians often describe periods of history from which few records have survived as **dark ages** – for instance, Europe after the fall of the Roman Empire. Some experts warn that a modern Dark Age has already begun, the result of storing records in ways that no one can read.

Dark Ages of Ancient Greece
c.1100BC-750BC

The time in between the end of the Bronze Age and the appearance of the first Greek city states.

Dark Ages in Europe
c.6th-10th centuries

The time in between the collapse of the Western Roman Empire and the founding of the Holy Roman Empire.

Dark Ages of Cambodia
c.1450-1863

The time in between the collapse of the Khmer Empire and the rise of modern Cambodia.

Digital Dark Age
1950s-present day

Since the invention of electronic computers, people have stored digital information on all sorts of devices, such as cassette tapes, floppy disks or CDs.

But computer technology changes very quickly, and most modern computers have no way to unlock the information stored on obsolete formats.

We are throwing all of our data into what could become an information black hole without realizing it.
(Internet pioneer, Vint Cerf)

33 Victorian wallpaper...

filled rooms with toxic dust and poison gas.

In 19th-century Europe, the invention of cheap new dyes made it possible for people to decorate their homes with vibrant hues. But their bold interior designs came with a hidden cost.

Pigments such as the wildly popular **Scheele's Green** and **Paris Green** were used on everything from children's toys to wallpaper.

By 1858, there were some **260 million km²** **(100 million square miles)** of Scheele's Green wallpaper in British homes.

A scrap of wallpaper the size of a handkerchief could contain a lethal dose of the toxic element **arsenic**.

In rooms papered with Scheele's Green, arsenic dust gradually powdered down from the walls

...and in leaky corners, chemical reactions released arsenic gas from the damp wallpaper.

Many people knew that arsenic wallpapers caused illnesses and deaths, but their production was never banned.

34 The Black Death spread...

up to 25 miles a day.

The Black Death was a disease, or plague, that devastated Europe, Asia and North Africa in the 14th century. It spread rapidly, killing half the population of Europe in just four years. There was no known cure.

Different forms of the plague spread in different ways:

One type spread to humans through bites from fleas that lived on black rats.

Another type was passed from person to person through the air.

Symptoms included fever, pain, spots and black boils – which gave the disease its name.

EUROPE

By land, the disease spread on average about 3km (2 miles) a day.

The Black Death spread by sea with astonishing speed. Ships sailed about 40km (25 miles) a day. Infected rats scurried onto ships and took the disease into new ports.

AFRICA

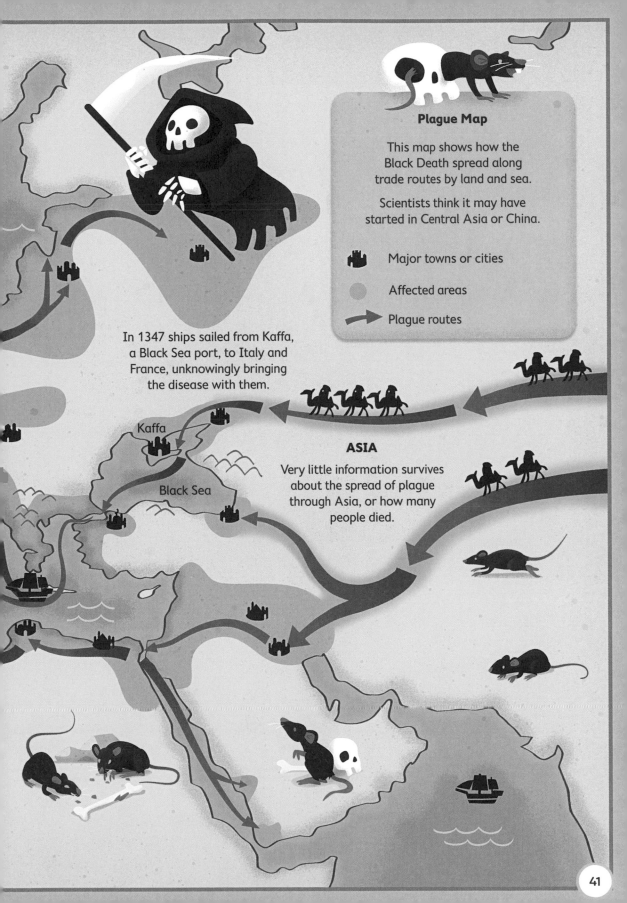

Plague Map

This map shows how the Black Death spread along trade routes by land and sea.

Scientists think it may have started in Central Asia or China.

🏰 Major towns or cities

⬤ Affected areas

➤ Plague routes

In 1347 ships sailed from Kaffa, a Black Sea port, to Italy and France, unknowingly bringing the disease with them.

Kaffa

Black Sea

ASIA

Very little information survives about the spread of plague through Asia, or how many people died.

35 In only a hundred years...

the speed of travel became ten times faster.

For most of human history, people could travel no further or faster than a horse could carry them. But, during the 19th century, new technology changed this forever, allowing people to cross oceans and continents in just a few days, by land, sea and even air.

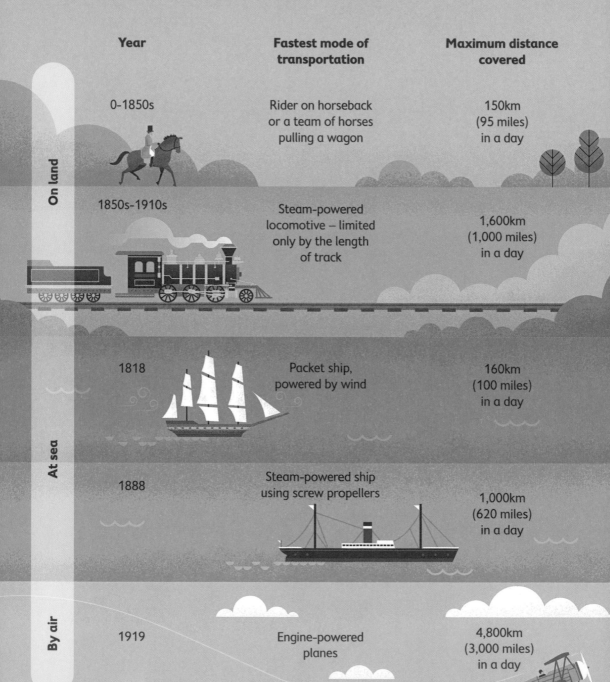

	Year	Fastest mode of transportation	Maximum distance covered
On land	0–1850s	Rider on horseback or a team of horses pulling a wagon	150km (95 miles) in a day
	1850s–1910s	Steam-powered locomotive – limited only by the length of track	1,600km (1,000 miles) in a day
At sea	1818	Packet ship, powered by wind	160km (100 miles) in a day
	1888	Steam-powered ship using screw propellers	1,000km (620 miles) in a day
By air	1919	Engine-powered planes	4,800km (3,000 miles) in a day

36 A race around the world...

tested fact against fiction.

On November 14, 1889, two journalists based in New York, USA, took part in a new kind of race, inspired by Jules Verne's novel, *Around the World in 80 Days*. They wanted to find out if the fictional journey was possible.

Elizabeth Bisland, sponsored by *Cosmopolitan* magazine, caught a train and headed west.

SAN FRANCISCO

Central Line to San Francisco

NEW YORK

Nellie Bly, sponsored by *New York World*, boarded a ship and headed east.

Augusta Victoria Arrives in Southampton, UK Nov 21

Both planned each stage of their journeys using a recent innovation — pre-printed timetables. Another new invention, the telegraph, allowed them to make international bookings.

At the halfway mark...

HONG KONG

Have you seen Elizabeth?

Sorry! She was here three days ago. Better hurry up...

Anxious for a good headline, the owner of the *New York World* paid for a private train...

NEW YORK

SAN FRANCISCO

...that whisked Bly across the USA in record time: just 69 hours.

Bly won the race, completing her journey in 72 days, 6 hours and 11 minutes — the fastest journey by far at the time. Bisland arrived back in 76 days and 12 hours, impeded by a slow Atlantic crossing — but still faster than the time limit of 80 days.

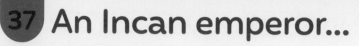

37 An Incan emperor...

filled a room with a gold.

In 1532, Atahualpa, ruler of the South American Inca Empire, was captured by Spanish adventurer Francisco Pizarro. Atahualpa offered to fill a room with gold, in return for his freedom.

Pizarro accepted Atahualpa's ransom offer. Soon, llamas laden with gold and silver made their way through the Andes mountains from far across the Inca empire.

The Incas brought over 6,000kg (13,200lb) of gold and more of silver. It was the largest ransom ever paid.

Pizarro took the treasure but still executed Atahualpa.

SOUTH AMERICA

Atahualpa's empire of 12 million people stretched along the Andes mountains of South America.

Inca ....▶ Empire

The Spanish eventually melted most of the gold and silver, turning it into bars or coins to be shipped back to Spain.

38 Tulip bulbs used to cost more...
than mansions.

In the early 17th century, tulips were new to Europe and very rare. Meanwhile, the United Provinces (now the Netherlands) had become the richest country in Europe. With cash to splash, the Dutch bought tulip bulbs and prices began to rise. This was the start of **tulip mania**.

At different times during tulip mania, one bulb cost the same as...

34 barrels of ale

454kg (1,000lb) of cheese

12 fat sheep

The cost of feeding a crew on a ship for a year.

1 extravagant mansion with coach house

But, in February 1637, the prices collapsed...

...because too many bulbs had been imported.

Buyers refused to pay the high prices that they had previously agreed to. Tulip mania was over.

39 Generals not privates...

were more likely to die in the American Civil War.

The American Civil War (1861–1865) was one of the bloodiest wars in history. On both sides, the most likely to die in combat were not the junior soldiers – known as **privates** – but officers with the rank of **brigadier general**, who led brigades onto the battlefields.

Total deaths during the war
(from combat and disease):

600,000 – 800,000

25%
of all soldiers died from
combat injuries.

33%
of all generals died
from combat injuries.

40 Bugs not bullets...

killed the most soldiers during the American Civil War.

Living in makeshift camps, many soldiers died from diseases such as pneumonia and dysentery. Both diseases spread through bacteria that grew in contaminated food and water.

Approx.
number of deaths from
combat injuries:

230,000

Approx. number of
war deaths caused
by disease:

400,000

41 Weavers smashed looms...

to fight for their rights.

In 1811, a secret society of textile workers in England, called the **Luddites**, made a series of night raids on factories. They smashed up mechanical looms and burned down mills, in protest against new machinery that threatened their jobs.

The Luddites were skilled knitters, weavers and spinners who previously worked at home or in small workshops.

They met at night to plan attacks on factories.

English poet, Lord Byron, fought for the Luddites in Parliament. But he was unable to stop harsh new laws to curb their protests.

The name "Luddite" may have come from a weaver named Ned Lud, one of the early protesters.

Many rioters were executed or sent to prison in Australia. The rebellion ended in 1816.

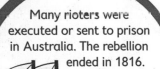

Over the next 100 years, machines led to an explosion of growth in many industries, a change known as the **Industrial Revolution**.

42 Germans helped a Russian...

to start a revolution.

In 1917, Germany was fighting the First World War on two fronts. Eager to end fighting against Russia in the east, German leaders helped exiled Russian revolutionary known as Lenin to return to Russia. They hoped that he would cause enough trouble to make Russia pull out of the war.

March 1917
Russia's ruler, the Tsar, stepped down after a mass uprising in Petrograd. A provisional government took over.

NORWAY

SWEDEN

Petrograd
(later named Leningrad, now St. Petersburg)

April 1917
Lenin, an exile in Zurich, Switzerland, returned to Russia in a train guarded by German troops.

Boat to Sweden

RUSSIAN EMPIRE

GERMANY

Lenin's eight-day train journey avoided areas where heavy fighting was taking place.

Zurich
SWITZERLAND

AUSTRIA-HUNGARY

November 1917
Lenin led an armed revolution that seized control of Russia's provisional government.

March 1918
As the Germans hoped, one of Lenin's first acts as leader was to end Russia's involvement in the First World War.

43 Lenin's body...

is re-embalmed every two years.

Lenin was hailed a hero for leading the Russian Revolution. He helped set up the world's first communist country – **the Soviet Union**, a vast group of states including Russia. After his death in 1924, his body was preserved, and is still on view in a mausoleum in Red Square, Moscow.

Lenin died aged 53, only seven years after the Revolution. His body was immediately preserved and is re-treated every two years by a team of scientists known as the **mausoleum group**.

Lenin briefly shared his mausoleum with the preserved body of his successor, Joseph Stalin, who died in 1953. However, Stalin was later denounced for his brutal rule and his body was removed.

44 A pirate and a queen parlayed...
in Latin.

In the 16th century, the English set out to conquer Ireland. One of the rebels against English rule was Gráinne Ní Mháille, a pirate raider and queen of the Connacht region. One of her last acts was to make a pact with her enemy, Queen Elizabeth I of England, but they did it in Latin.

In the 1560s, Gráinne began rebelling against English rule by raiding English-held posts with her ships.

After nearly 30 years, the English governor of Connacht seized Gráinne's land and took her son prisoner. In 1593, Gráinne sailed up the Thames to plead her case to Elizabeth. Neither spoke the other's language, but both knew Latin, the language of educated people in Europe.

I have nothing left to lose! Your majesty, I will swear loyalty to you if you return my land and son!

An Irish pirate queen, eh? Still, we queens are few and far between! I return your land and son to you!

Ireland

England

Gráinne lived as a pirate for the rest of her life.
Both queens died, months apart, in 1603.

45 Christmas trees...

were once a celebrity trend.

The tradition of indoor Christmas trees began in Germany in the 16th century. It took off in other countries in the 1850s, after magazines showed pictures of British monarch, Queen Victoria, with a Christmas tree.

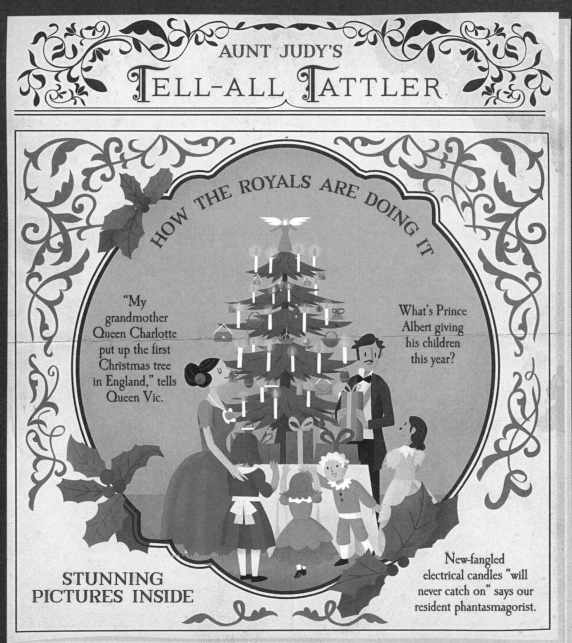

AUNT JUDY'S

TELL-ALL TATTLER

HOW THE ROYALS ARE DOING IT

"My grandmother Queen Charlotte put up the first Christmas tree in England," tells Queen Vic.

What's Prince Albert giving his children this year?

STUNNING PICTURES INSIDE

New-fangled electrical candles "will never catch on" says our resident phantasmagorist.

Pictures of the Queen's Christmas tree were published across the British Empire every year for decades.

Now, in the 21st century, more than 100 million households around the world put up a Christmas tree.

46 The Roman Empire...

was only the 23rd largest in history.

An **empire** is a collection of territories and countries, all controlled by a single leader or government. It's impossible to determine which empire has been the most powerful or influential, but one thing historians can say is which covered the greatest area.

Many empires experienced major upheavals within their lifetimes. The dates on this page show the eras when each was at its largest.

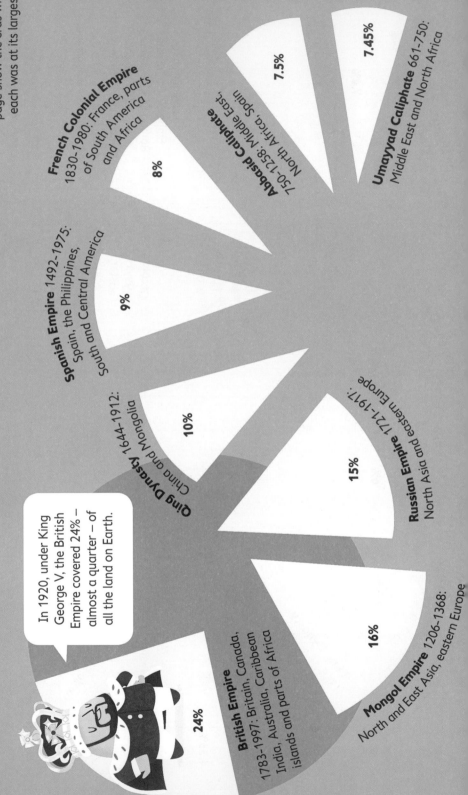

French Colonial Empire 1830-1980: France, parts of South America and Africa — 8%

Abbasid Caliphate 750-1258: Middle East, North Africa, Spain — 7.5%

Umayyad Caliphate 661-750: Middle East and North Africa — 7.45%

Spanish Empire 1492-1975: Spain, the Philippines, South and Central America — 9%

Qing Dynasty 1644-1912: China and Mongolia — 10%

Russian Empire 1721-1917: North Asia and eastern Europe — 15%

Mongol Empire 1206-1368: North and East Asia, eastern Europe — 16%

British Empire 1783-1997: Britain, Canada, Caribbean islands and parts of Africa, India, Australia — 24%

In 1920, under King George V, the British Empire covered 24% – almost a quarter – of all the land on Earth.

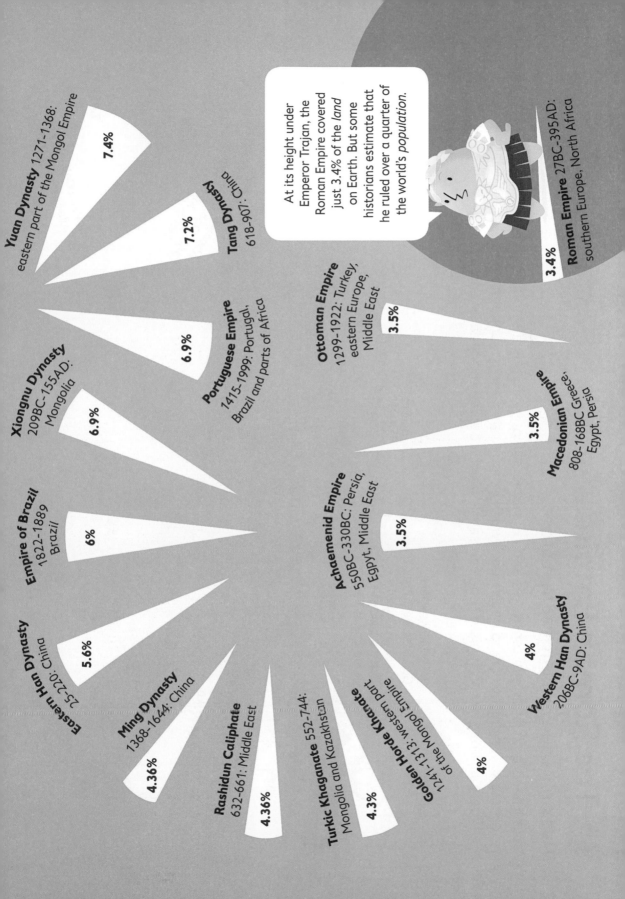

Yuan Dynasty 1271-1368: eastern part of the Mongol Empire
7.4%

Tang Dynasty 618-907: China
7.2%

Portuguese Empire 1415-1999: Portugal, Brazil and parts of Africa
6.9%

Xiongnu Dynasty 209BC-155AD: Mongolia
6.9%

Empire of Brazil 1822-1889 Brazil
6%

Eastern Han Dynasty 25-220: China
5.6%

Ming Dynasty 1368-1644: China
4.36%

Rashidun Caliphate 632-661: Middle East
4.36%

Turkic Khaganate 552-744: Mongolia and Kazakhstan
4.3%

Golden Horde Khanate 1241-1313: western part of the Mongol Empire
4.3%

Western Han Dynasty 206BC-9AD: China
4%

Achaemenid Empire 550BC-330BC: Persia, Egypt, Middle East
3.5%

Macedonian Empire 808-168BC Greece, Egypt, Persia
3.5%

Ottoman Empire 1299-1922: Turkey, eastern Europe, Middle East
3.5%

Roman Empire 27BC-395AD: southern Europe, North Africa
3.4%

At its height under Emperor Trajan, the Roman Empire covered just 3.4% of the *land* on Earth. But some historians estimate that he ruled over a quarter of the world's *population*.

47 The world's most valuable dye...

was made from rotten sea snails.

For thousands of years, the only way to get purple dye was from the decomposing bodies of sea snails. It was produced almost exclusively by people living on the east coast of the Mediterranean, who were known as the **Phoenicians**.

Phoenicians began making the dye in around 1500BC.

It came from sea snails called *murex*, once plentiful on the Mediterranean coast.

In Tyre, the main port of Phoenicia, there were many murex pits, where the snails were left to rot, producing their precious dye.

It took **12,000** rotten murex snails to produce enough dye to cover a handkerchief-sized piece of fabric.

The dye was worth its own weight in silver. Only wealthy people could afford to wear clothes with purple trim, and only the wealthiest of all dressed entirely in purple.

48 A king gave away so much gold...

he caused an economic meltdown.

Musa Keita I, *mansa* – or ruler – of the Mali Empire in the 14th century, owned more gold than could be counted. His wealth came from mines in Mali, and from territories he conquered in surrounding lands in West Africa.

A devout Muslim, Musa began a pilgrimage to the holy city of Mecca in 1324. As part of his pilgrimage, Musa gave gold to many people he met along the way, and paid for several new mosques to be built.

Cairo

Medina

Mecca

Mali Empire

Timbuktu

Charity is God's will.

All of a sudden, lots of people owned lots of gold, making every single gold coin less valuable.

Shopkeepers began to sell their goods for higher and higher prices, creating a crisis known as **hyperinflation**.

Then people couldn't afford to buy things or pay off debts, because no one wanted any more gold.

Sorry, everyone.

On his way back to Mali, Musa bought back much of his gold. Over the following decades, this eventually solved the crisis.

made a one-day journey last eight years.

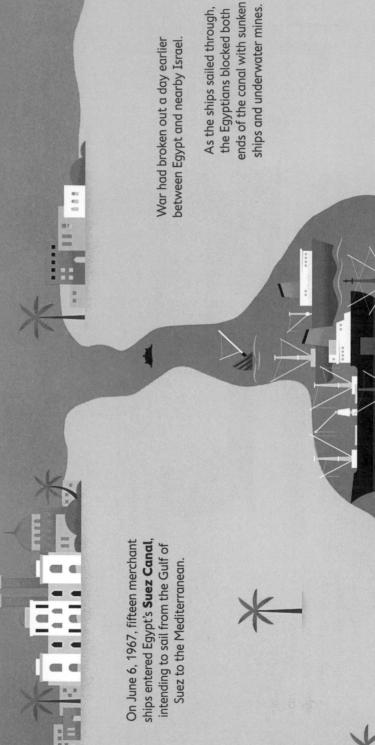

Mediterranean Sea

On June 6, 1967, fifteen merchant ships entered Egypt's **Suez Canal**, intending to sail from the Gulf of Suez to the Mediterranean.

War had broken out a day earlier between Egypt and nearby Israel.

As the ships sailed through, the Egyptians blocked both ends of the canal with sunken ships and underwater mines.

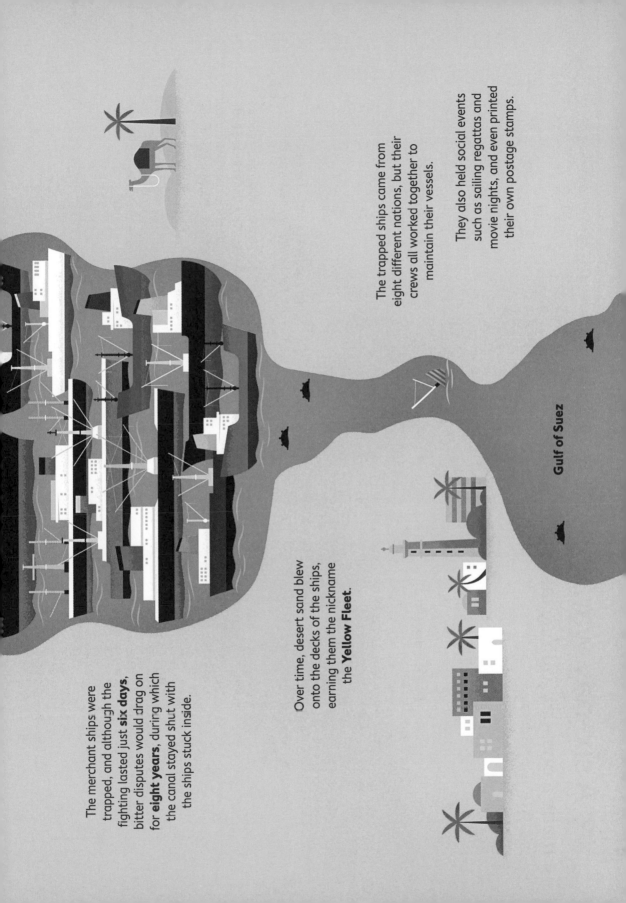

The merchant ships were trapped, and although the fighting lasted just **six days**, bitter disputes would drag on for **eight years**, during which the canal stayed shut with the ships stuck inside.

Over time, desert sand blew onto the decks of the ships, earning them the nickname the **Yellow Fleet.**

The trapped ships came from eight different nations, but their crews all worked together to maintain their vessels.

They also held social events such as sailing regattas and movie nights, and even printed their own postage stamps.

Gulf of Suez

50 A midnight snack...

used to be a regular habit.

Medieval texts sometimes refer to "first" and "second" sleeps. Some historians believe this is evidence that it used to be typical for people to have two bedtimes each night.

Dusk

Dawn

First sleep

Second sleep

6pm

11pm

1am

6am

In between sleeps, people relaxed, by eating a snack, chatting, reading (if they knew how) or praying.

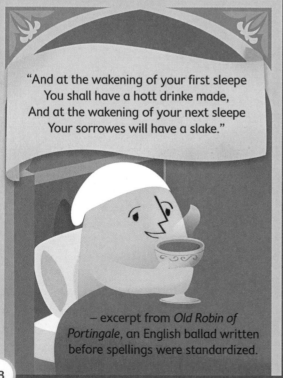

"And at the wakening of your first sleepe
You shall have a hott drinke made,
And at the wakening of your next sleepe
Your sorrowes will have a slake."

– excerpt from *Old Robin of Portingale*, an English ballad written before spellings were standardized.

Christian and Muslim prayer books detailed prayers that should be used during the night-time waking period.

By the 18th century, references to first and second sleeps became far less common. Most people today sleep for a single, long session.

51 Deep-sea drones...

make great archaeologists.

Some of the best-preserved relics from ancient times are found at the bottom of the sea, in areas known as **anoxic zones**. Water in these zones contains very little oxygen, and it's too dangerous for human divers to swim in. Instead, deep-sea drones are sent in to explore.

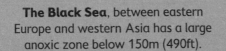

The Black Sea, between eastern Europe and western Asia has a large anoxic zone below 150m (490ft).

Underwater archaeologists can explore shallower coastal areas of the Black Sea. But to chart the anoxic zone, they send in drone submersibles, known as **ROVs** (Remotely Operated Vehicles).

In normal sea water, wood, rope and even metal will rot or corrode, causing entire ships to disintegrate.

In the Black Sea's anoxic zone, 1,500-year-old ships are so well preserved that ROVs have photographed intact rigging, and even chisel marks, still visible on wooden hulls.

Walking can change the world...

if you have enough comrades.

Across the last 100 years, people in countries around the world have helped bring about changes in the law, and even toppled kings and governments, by the simple act of gathering together and marching.

POWER TO THE PEOPLE

Women's Day Strike
St. Petersburg, Russia
March 8, 1917

200,000 people went on strike for two days, protesting against war and supporting a growing revolution.

Within a few days, the strikers were joined by the Russian Army, who helped them overthrow Tsar Nicholas II.

The Salt March
Dandi, British-ruled India
March 1930

30,000-60,000 people walked from Ahmedabad to Dandi to collect salt – illegal by British law.

Thousands were arrested – but the march helped gain international support for India's wish to become independent from Britain.

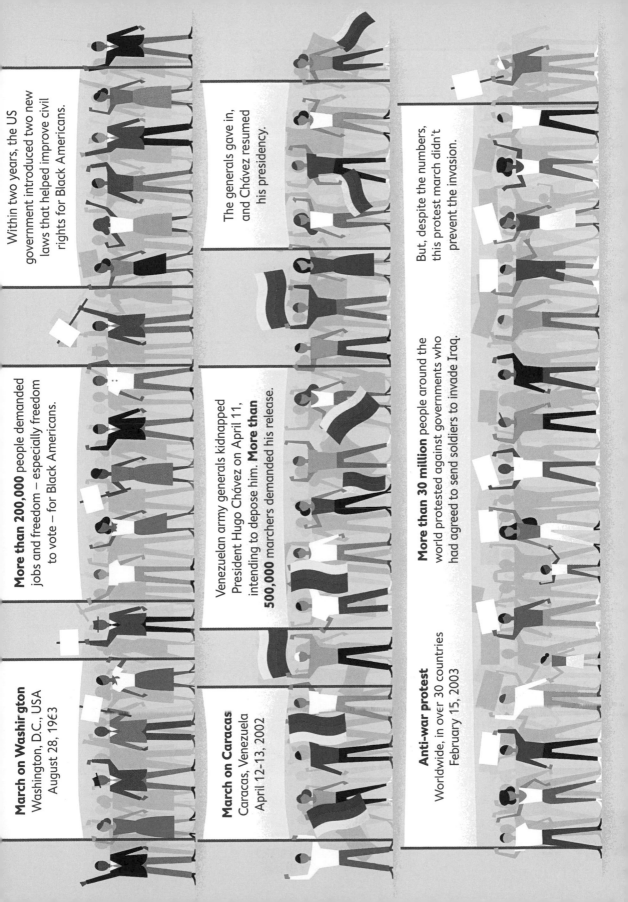

March on Washington
Washington, D.C., USA
August 28, 1963

More than 200,000 people demanded jobs and freedom – especially freedom to vote – for Black Americans.

Within two years, the US government introduced two new laws that helped improve civil rights for Black Americans.

March on Caracas
Caracas, Venezuela
April 12-13, 2002

Venezuelan army generals kidnapped President Hugo Chávez on April 11, intending to depose him. **More than 500,000** marchers demanded his release.

The generals gave in, and Chávez resumed his presidency.

Anti-war protest
Worldwide, in over 30 countries
February 15, 2003

More than 30 million people around the world protested against governments who had agreed to send soldiers to invade Iraq.

But, despite the numbers, this protest march didn't prevent the invasion.

53 Warriors without a war...

still had to be ready for battle.

In the early 17th century, Tokugawa Ieyasu became ruler of Japan and helped usher in over 200 years of peace. An entire class or warriors, known as *samurai*, never fought again – but they still had to wear ceremonial battle dress on occasion, handing it down through the generations.

Full samurai battle dress required more than **30** separate pieces of clothing and equipment.

Around **10%** of all Japanese men were born as samurai, until the title was officially abolished in 1863.

54 An army lay hidden...

for over two thousand years.

In 1974, farmers digging a well broke into an ancient burial chamber. They discovered an army of at least **8,000** soldiers, and hundreds of entertainers, all made from terracotta – a kind of clay. They had been buried in 206BC alongside the body of Qin Shi Huang, first emperor of China.

Emperor Qin Shi Huang commissioned the tomb when he was still a teenager.

Legends say he wanted his afterlife to be exactly as his life on Earth – guarded by an army, but also surrounded by entertainers.

Each figure is life size, has its own unique face, and is hand-painted.

Writing from Qin's time did not record the tomb's exact location, which remained a mystery until 1974.

Even today, one vault remains sealed, to preserve its contents – likely to include the Emperor's own tomb.

55 Bird droppings helped start a war...

in South America.

In the 19th century, the best fertilizer in the world was **guano**, the dried droppings of sea birds, mined on desert coasts and remote islands, such as Peru's Chincha Islands. It was rare, and rare meant expensive – expensive enough to fight over.

I'm a Guanay Cormorant. My friends and I make a lot of this guano.

All this white stuff is guano. Underneath is rock.

Coming out of the bird is wet guano.

Until the 19th century, much of South America was ruled by Spain. The people of Peru had claimed independence in 1826, but this wasn't recognized by the Spanish government, causing tension between the two.

We're Peruvians and we mine the guano here. Guano sales make up **70%** of Peru's money.

56 The tallest temple in the world...
was also a to-do list.

Built in the 660s, a pagoda at the heart of a temple complex known as **Hwangnyongsa**, in Korea, was the tallest wooden structure in the world. At the time, it was taller than any building except the great pyramids of Egypt.

The pagoda was commissioned by Queen Seondeok of Silla before she died in 647.

In 632, she had conquered the kingdom of Baekji, uniting communities across the Korean peninsula.

Each floor of the pagoda was said to represent one of nine kingdoms in the region.

Under my rule

- Kingdom 9 — 9. ☐
- Kingdom 8 — 8. ☐
- Kingdom 7 — 7. ☐
- Kingdom 6 — 6. ☐
- Kingdom 5 — 5. ☐
- Kingdom 4 — 4. ☐
- Kingdom 3 — 3. ☐
- Baekji — 2. ☑
- Silla — 1. ☑

I am destined to rule over *all* of the kingdoms, not just those I already possess.

Unfortunately, Seondeok died before she could conquer any more kingdoms. The entire temple complex was burned down by Mongol invaders in the 13th century so historians are unsure what the other seven kingdoms were.

A gift of parrot's eggs...

could unseat an emperor.

In the 17th and 18th centuries, the Oyo Empire (in what is now Nigeria), was governed by a succession of rulers known as **alaafins**. They reigned over all the other, lesser kings in the empire. A detailed system of checks and balances helped prevent abuse, based around the giving of a gift...

Alaafin – absolute ruler whose power came from the gods [1]

Aremo – eldest son of the Alaafin – a figure of great authority and power [2]

Oyo Mesi – supreme council of seven nobles who advised and served the Alaafin [3]

Ogboni – secret fraternity respected for their wisdom and religious authority [4]

If the Oyo Mesi offered the Alaafin a dish of parrot's eggs, this meant his subjects (and his ancestors) rejected him, and he had to commit suicide.

[1] *Held power only as long as he upheld traditions and kept the support of the Oyo Mesi*
[2] *Could never become alaafin: when his father died, he was expected to commit suicide*
[3] *Could depose the Alaafin if they felt he was unsuitable; also responsible for electing a new Alaafin among candidates from several royal bloodlines*
[4] *Could overrule the Oyo Mesi; represented the traditions and will of the people*

58 Athenian democracy...

wasn't very democratic.

The ancient Greek city state Athens is famous for being the birthplace of democracy, over 2,500 years ago. Democracy means the right of the people to decide how the state is run, but in Athens not everyone counted as *the people*.

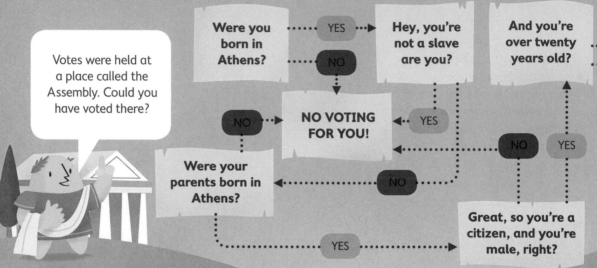

Votes were held at a place called the Assembly. Could you have voted there?

Were you born in Athens? ······ YES ···▶ Hey, you're not a slave are you?

······ NO

And you're over twenty years old?

NO ···▶ NO VOTING FOR YOU! ◀··· YES

NO ▶ YES

Were your parents born in Athens? ◀·············· NO ·····

NO ·····

Great, so you're a citizen, and you're male, right?

······ YES ··············▶

59 Votes for women...

came thousands of years after votes for men.

Over 2,500 years ago Athens, in Greece, became the first place to hold elections. But women weren't allowed to vote in Greece until 1952. Here are some dates when women were first able to vote in different countries.

1893 **New Zealand**	1902 **Australia**	1906 **Finland**	1917 **Canada**
First country to let women vote. Women stood to become politicians from 1919.	Native Aboriginal women couldn't vote until 1962. First woman elected 1921.	First European country to let women vote. First woman in any parliament in 1907.	Indigenous First Nations women didn't get the vote until 1960.

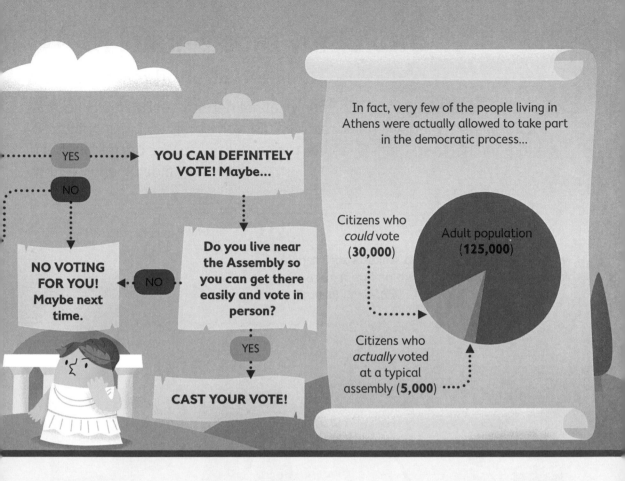

YES ┈┈┈▶ **YOU CAN DEFINITELY VOTE! Maybe...**

NO

NO VOTING FOR YOU! Maybe next time. ◀┈ NO ┈ **Do you live near the Assembly so you can get there easily and vote in person?**

YES

CAST YOUR VOTE!

In fact, very few of the people living in Athens were actually allowed to take part in the democratic process...

Citizens who *could* vote (**30,000**)

Adult population (**125,000**)

Citizens who *actually* voted at a typical assembly (**5,000**)

**1920
USA**
In some states, Black American women couldn't vote until 1965.

**1929
Ecuador**
First country in South America to let women vote.

**1930
South Africa**
White women could vote, but Black women couldn't vote until 1994.

**1945
Senegal and Togo**
First countries in Africa to let women of all races vote.

**2015
Saudi Arabia**
Women could vote and stand for election. Female candidates had to stand behind a screen.

Women's rights...

were greater in ancient Egypt than Victorian Britain.

Egypt
3100BC to 300AD

UK
up to 1882

Jobs: A woman could be anything from a servant to a high priestess. Some studied for professions, such as medicine.

Jobs: Many women worked as servants, in factories and on farms – but they were barred from studying at universities and could not be priests.

Dress: Dresses were light, loose fitting and comfortable.

Dress: Women wore heavy clothing over tight corsets that greatly restricted movement.

Marriage and property: Women could own property in their own name, and keep it after divorce or a husband's death. Married women received property to support them after a husband's death.

Marriage and property: Women had to obey their husbands. Until the *Married Women's Property Act* in 1882, everything a married woman owned passed to her husband. Widows were often left very poorly off.

Divorce: Either partner could divorce the other with a declaration. Women usually gained control of the children.

Divorce: This required an act of parliament, and only wealthy men could afford this. Women lost all rights to their children.

Both Egyptian and Victorian women could become rulers.

61 Brazil has more Black citizens...

than any African country except Nigeria.

From the 15th to the 19th century, more than **10 million** people, mostly West Africans, were enslaved, bought by Europeans and shipped across the Atlantic to the Americas. **Four million** of those slaves went to Brazil and today, **100 million** of the **200 million** people in Brazil descend from them.

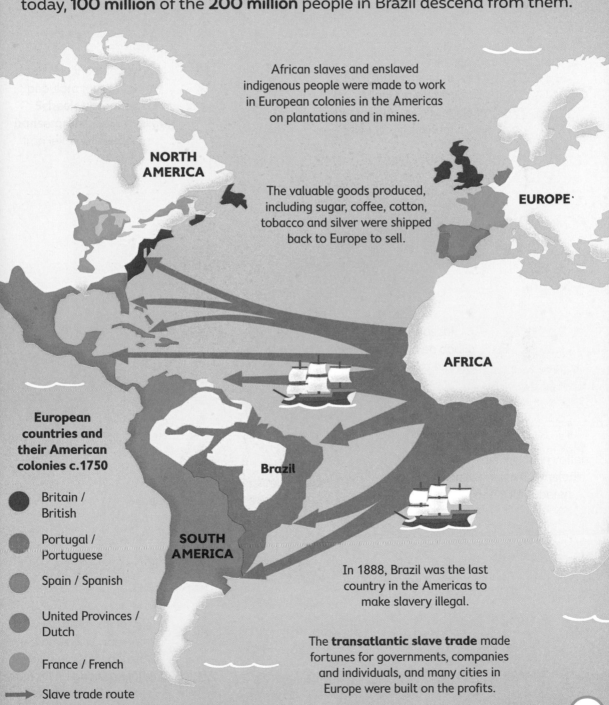

African slaves and enslaved indigenous people were made to work in European colonies in the Americas on plantations and in mines.

NORTH AMERICA

The valuable goods produced, including sugar, coffee, cotton, tobacco and silver were shipped back to Europe to sell.

EUROPE

AFRICA

European countries and their American colonies c.1750

- Britain / British
- Portugal / Portuguese
- Spain / Spanish
- United Provinces / Dutch
- France / French
- ➝ Slave trade route

Brazil

SOUTH AMERICA

In 1888, Brazil was the last country in the Americas to make slavery illegal.

The **transatlantic slave trade** made fortunes for governments, companies and individuals, and many cities in Europe were built on the profits.

62 A single Polynesian canoe...

could carry an entire civilization.

Polynesia is a vast region of the Pacific Ocean, made up of more than **1,000** widely scattered islands, including Hawai'i, New Zealand, and Rapa Nui. These were settled one by one, by people arriving in canoes, over a period of many hundreds of years, beginning around 3,500 years ago.

When Polynesian settlers first set sail to remote islands, they didn't know what they might find there. So they packed their canoes with farm animals and **canoe plants**: roots, seeds and cuttings of all the plants their civilization depended on.

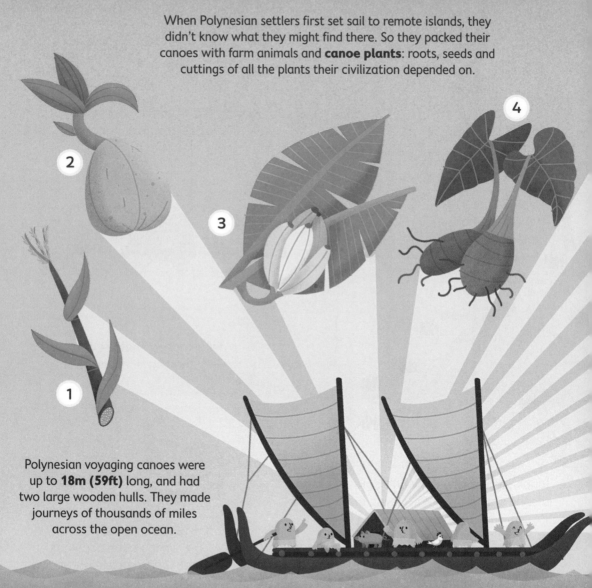

Polynesian voyaging canoes were up to **18m (59ft)** long, and had two large wooden hulls. They made journeys of thousands of miles across the open ocean.

Here is a list of some of the most common canoe plants and their uses:
1. Sugar cane – medicine, sweetener **2. Coconut palm** – food, water, ropes, sails, building material, containers **3. Banana** – food, building material **4. Taro** – main source of food
5. Yam – food **6. Bamboo** – tools, musical instruments, building material, containers

The Polynesians knew that, wherever they landed, they could use their canoe plants to grow whatever they needed.

The plants could provide everything from food and medicine to materials for making rope, roofing, flutes and drums — and even new canoes.

7. Sweet potato – food **8. Breadfruit** – food, medicine, chewing gum, building material, clothing, glue **9. Wild ginger** – food, medicine, shampoo **10. Turmeric** – spice, medicine, dye
11. Polynesian arrowroot – food **12. Bottle gourd** – containers, musical instruments
13. Candlenut tree – lamp oil, candles, medicine, food, dye, canoe-building material

63 A palace fortress in the sky...
could not save a Sri Lankan king.

Kashyapa I became King of Sri Lanka in the year 477 after murdering his father. But he feared attack from his brother, Moggallana, the rightful heir, so Kashyapa built a palace in the safest place he could find...

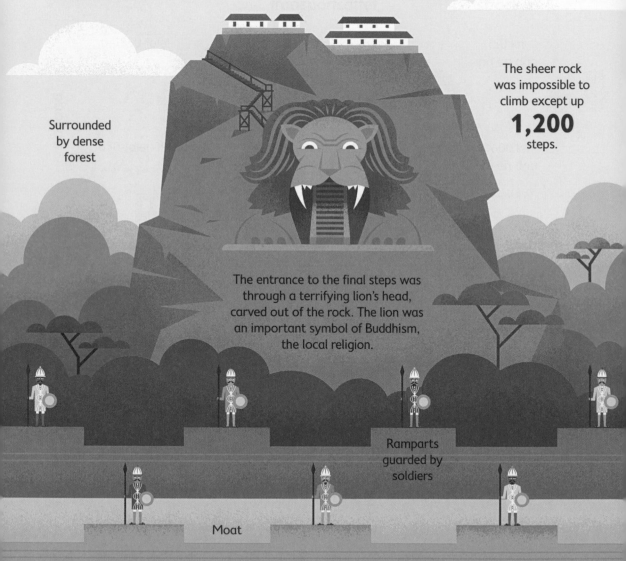

Sihagiri – Lion rock
200m (660ft) high

360° view for keeping watch for approaching enemy armies

The sheer rock was impossible to climb except up
1,200 steps.

Surrounded by dense forest

The entrance to the final steps was through a terrifying lion's head, carved out of the rock. The lion was an important symbol of Buddhism, the local religion.

Ramparts guarded by soldiers

Moat

After 18 years, Kashyapa's army turned against him. Kashyapa killed himself, and Moggallana became king.

Moggallana abandoned the rock palace. It became a Buddhist monastery until the 14th century.

64 Monks stole the secret...

of silk-making from China.

In the early 6th century, silk was an expensive luxury cloth, made primarily in China, where the method for making it was a closely guarded secret. The key was a kind of caterpillar called a silkworm, that fed on mulberry leaves. As silkworms mature, they spin a cocoon of long, fine silk thread that silk makers weave on a loom to make silk cloth.

Eager to learn the secrets of silk, Justinian I, ruler of the Byzantine Empire, sent two monks to China in the year 553.

The monks stole silkworm eggs and mulberry seeds and smuggled them out of China in hollow bamboo canes.

They taught Justinian the secret method for breeding silkworms and making silk.

Emperor Justinian set up silk factories in several cities and the Byzantine Empire grew rich, trading its silk in Europe.

65 The population of Europe...
has halved at least twice in the last 2,000 years.

Some diseases are so infectious they can spread rapidly across continents, creating outbreaks known as **pandemics**. Two of the worst killed more than half the population of Europe, as well as devastating populations across Asia.

2

**1346-1352
Black Death**

1

**541-546
Plague of Justinian**

A deadly disease known as bubonic plague spread from North Africa to the Middle East and much of Europe.

Bubonic plague returned again, this time spreading from Asia to Europe and North Africa.

In Europe alone, around **half** of all people in cities and **one third** of all people in the countryside were killed.

The same disease returned every few decades until the year 750.

Accurate figures are impossible to find, but the Black Death may have killed over **200 million** people in Europe alone.

Smaller outbreaks of bubonic plague returned to some parts of the world over the next five centuries.

Estimated population of the world in the year 1: **170 million**

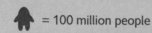 = 100 million people

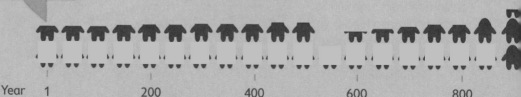

Year   1   200   400   600   800

66 The population of the world...

has quadrupled in the last century.

Historians estimate that the global population in 1900 was **1.6 billion**. A hundred years later it had swelled to **6.1 billion**...

It's projected that by the year 2050 the global population will be **10 billion**.

Fitter, stronger, healthier

Many factors have contributed to the rapid rise in population:

- improvements in medicine
- awareness of the importance of hygiene
- better diet

The more people who survive into adulthood, the more people are able to have children, helping the population rise very rapidly.

Births and deaths

In the US, between 1900 and 1975, the number of women who died as a result of childbirth went down by **99%**.

In the same period, the number of babies who died in their first year went down by over **90%**.

By 2001, the rest of the world had caught up.

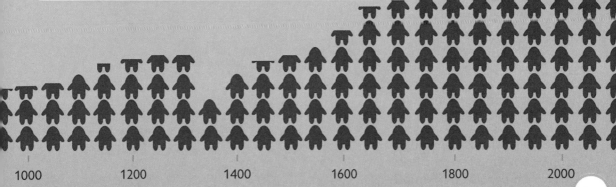

| 1000 | 1200 | 1400 | 1600 | 1800 | 2000 |

67 A pharaoh was almost erased...

from recorded history.

Hatshepsut, whose name means *foremost of noble ladies*, ruled Egypt around 3,500 years ago. Not only was she one of a few female pharaohs, she also opened up trade routes and commissioned vast building projects across Egypt. But modern historians almost didn't know she existed...

The pharaoh who came after Hatshepsut was her stepson, Tuthmosis III. Her family had a stronger claim to the throne than his. So, twenty years after her death, he gave orders to remove her name from inscriptions on buildings constructed for her. Here are some of the methods people tried:

SCRATCHING, CHIPPING OR SMOOTHING HER IMAGE OFF WALLS

COVERING OVER HER IMAGE WITH NEW BRICKS

CROSSING OUT HER NAME AND WRITING TUTHMOSIS III

DESTROYING THE BRICKS COMPLETELY

TUTHMOSIS III
~~HATSHEPSUT~~
WOZ ERE

It wasn't until over 3,000 years later that Egyptologists began to piece together her reign from what was left.

68 An admiral's body...
was stored in a barrel of brandy.

When British Vice Admiral Horatio Nelson died at sea during the Battle of Trafalgar in 1805, the ship's surgeon stored his body in brandy. This was to keep it from rotting on the six-week voyage home.

Sailors were torn between mourning their leader, and celebrating victory over France and Spain at the Battle of Trafalgar.

Nelson's body was displayed in a coffin for three days in London. **100,000** people lined up to see his body before the funeral.

In those days, most sailors who died in battle were buried at sea.

Their bodies were sewn up in heavy canvas, weighted with iron chains and slid overboard.

69 Ancient storytellers...

had to know their stories by heart.

Before people started writing stories down, storytellers memorized them to recite, and teach to the next generation of performers. These stories existed for hundreds of years before they were ever written down.

Here are some of the most famous stories from around the world. These are all **myths**. Myths are an early kind of history. Although they aren't exactly true, they show how people long ago viewed the past. The stories were composed as poems or songs with repeated rhythms to make them easier to remember.

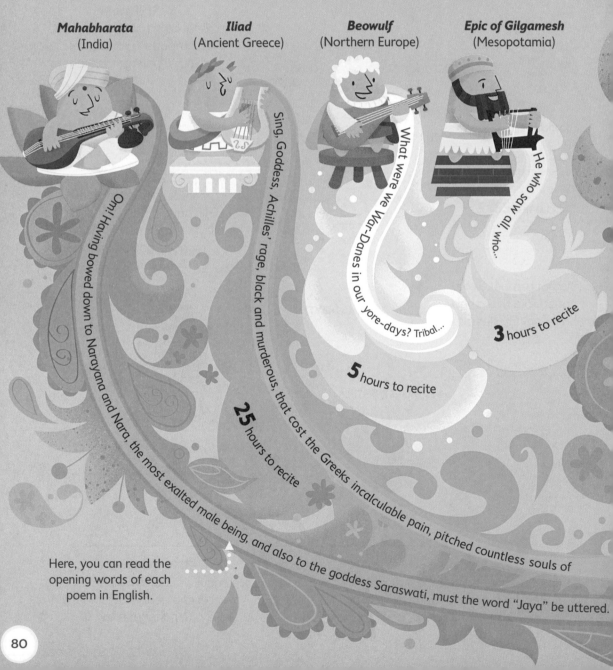

Mahabharata
(India)

Iliad
(Ancient Greece)

Beowulf
(Northern Europe)

Epic of Gilgamesh
(Mesopotamia)

Sing, Goddess, Achilles' rage, black and murderous, that cost the Greeks incalculable pain, pitched countless souls of

What were we War-Danes in our yore-days? Tribal...

He who saw all, who...

Om! Having bowed down to Narayana and Nara, the most exalted male being, and also to the goddess Saraswati, must the word "Jaya" be uttered.

3 hours to recite

5 hours to recite

25 hours to recite

Here, you can read the opening words of each poem in English.

Epic of Gilgamesh

Composed around 3,000 years ago

The people of Uruk hate their king, Gilgamesh. The gods create Enkidu, a wild man, to teach him a lesson, but Gilgamesh and Enkidu become friends...

Beowulf

Composed between 1,500 and 1,100 years ago

The hero Beowulf goes to fight the monster Grendel and save the people of King Hrothgar. But he doesn't bargain on Grendel's mother getting involved...

In 2015, 20 previously lost lines of the Gilgamesh were found on a 2,000-year-old tablet from Iraq.

Mahabharata

Composed between 2,900 and 1,600 years ago

Two sides of the great Kuru family, the Kaurava and Pandava, want the throne of Hastinapura. Will the Kurukshetra War decide their fates once and for all?

Iliad

Composed around 2,800 years ago

In the last year of the Trojan War, the Greeks can't decide whether to return a Trojan girl to her father, a priest of the god Apollo. Apollo is angry and so are the other gods...

heroes into Hades' dark...

350 hours to recite the whole poem — that's two weeks of continuous chanting.

Ugrasrava, the son of Lomaharshana, surnamed Sauti, which were...

Storytellers added to and changed the stories they performed. Because of this it's very hard to say when the stories were first composed. Historians can't agree on dates for *any* of them.

turned garbage into gold.

The problem of how to manage waste has troubled people throughout history. So much garbage has piled up, of so many different types, that societies have tried out many disposal methods, and even created some very unusual jobs to deal with it...

c.6600BC
Oldest known town waste pit, in Baran Höyük, Turkey

c.2100BC
Oldest record of official trash collection, in Heracleopolis, Egypt

c.2000BC
Oldest known recycling plant, for bronze, in China

1870s
The first **destructors** – giant furnaces to incinerate waste – were built. But the smoke and ashes covered local towns.

1875
Oldest known bins used for street collection, in London, UK

1938
First garbage truck with a built-in compactor to crush waste.

Present day
The vast majority of all waste is either buried or burned – just as it was 4,000 years ago. In the US, around **30%** of all waste is made up of packaging.

c.500BC
Oldest known laws about waste disposal, in Athens, Greece

c.1035
Oldest known disposable packaging – paper wrappings used in Cairo spice market

c.1200
Towns in Europe began raking up their waste, after it was linked to the spread of disease.

19th century
Large cities, especially in the US, hired pigs to eat all the garbage.

18th century
Scavengers, known as **mudlarks** and **toshers**, made money collecting and selling really filthy waste – including dog mess (used to purify leather).

c.1400s-1600s
Wealthy Europeans took to carrying **pomanders** – boxes of nice-smelling things – to cover up the smell of rotting waste.

Nowadays, digging up the things that people threw away gives archaeologists a valuable insight into how ordinary people used to live.

71 Red trousers...

killed thousands of Frenchmen in 1914.

When the First World War began in August 1914, French soldiers marched into battle wearing a traditional uniform of bright blue coats and vivid red trousers. Advances in weaponry meant that rifles and artillery were more accurate over greater distances than in previous wars. This meant the French were easy targets.

French soldier in 1914

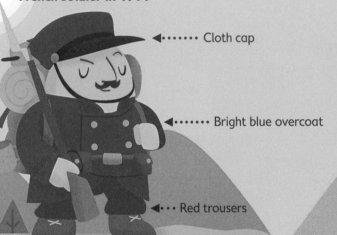

◄······· Cloth cap

◄······· Bright blue overcoat

◄··· Red trousers

Many men died before the French army adapted, gradually replacing the vibrant blues and reds with a less visible blue cloth.

Why red trousers?
People knew before the war that red trousers were highly visible – but wearing them was also felt to be patriotic, and so new, more camouflaged styles were rejected.

French soldier in 1918

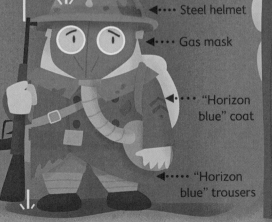

◄···· Steel helmet

◄···· Gas mask

◄···· "Horizon blue" coat

◄······ "Horizon blue" trousers

But it wasn't just the uniforms...
New weapons, such as machine guns, heavy artillery, gas, airplanes and tanks, changed the way wars were fought, and forced dramatic changes to military equipment and tactics, too.

72 Fighter pilots flipped bombs...

to knock them out of the sky.

During the Second World War, the German Air Force sent unmanned flying bombs, known as **V-1s**, over the sea to explode in British cities. British fighter pilots discovered a dangerous but reliable way to stop the bombs – literally nudging them with their wings.

Fighter planes used to seek and destroy bombs were known as **interceptors**.

Spitfire

V-1 bomb

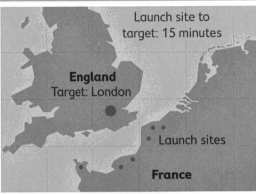
Launch site to target: 15 minutes

England
Target: London

Launch sites

France

Pilots aimed to fly alongside a bomb...

match its speed...

...then flip its wings from underneath.

This knocked the bomb into a spin. Most were sent crashing into the sea or into empty fields.

Many pilots preferred this method of tackling the bombs. Shooting them down risked pilots getting caught in the resulting explosion.

A combination of ground gunners and interceptor pilots meant that only **1 in 5** V-1s hit their targets.

73 A human chain...

spanned three countries.

In 1989, **two million** people held hands, making a very long human chain that stretched from Estonia to Lithuania. The chain was a peaceful protest by people who wanted independence from the Soviet Union.

Lithuania, Latvia and Estonia had been absorbed by the Soviet Union in 1940.

Tallinn, ESTONIA

For 15 minutes, people held hands. The chain was **676km (420 miles)** long.

Riga, LATVIA

The chain symbolized a common aim shared by three countries that all wanted independence.

Within seven months of the protest, Lithuania declared independence. Estonia and Latvia soon followed, and by the end of 1991, the Soviet Union had been dissolved.

Vilnius, LITHUANIA

Mammoths and pharaohs...

walked the Earth at the same time.

In 2560BC...

The last known population of woolly mammoths roamed across Wrangel Island (Russia) on the Arctic Ocean.

The city of Mohenjo-Daro in the Indus River Valley (Pakistan) was flourishing, with over 40,000 inhabitants and an advanced sewage system.

The massive central stones were erected at the monument of Stonehenge in England.

The Great Pyramid of Giza, constructed for the Egyptian pharaoh Khufu, was completed.

Over 30 types of gladiators...

fought in ancient Rome.

One of the most popular entertainments in ancient Rome was watching trained fighters, called gladiators, attack each other – or wild animals – in spectacular contests. Many styles were invented with different weapons and costumes, each with their own name.

Here are some of the main styles. Different types of gladiators would not usually fight at the same time.

Murmillones
wore helmets with fish fins on the crest, and had a large shield and sword.

Retiarii
fought with a trident, dagger and net, often against Murmillones.

Gladiatrices
female gladiators (shield and sword but no helmet)

Essedarii
fought with spears from chariots.

The greatest Roman arena was the **Colosseum** in Rome. Begun in the year 70, it seated **50,000** spectators. Beneath the arena was a maze of underground tunnels and cages for wild animals.

76 Peasants beat businessmen...

in 17th-century Japan.

Throughout history, each society developed its own social structure. In Japan, for example, during the Edo period (1603–1868), businessmen such as merchants and shopkeepers – however rich they were – had the lowest position in society, lower than even the poorest peasants. This wasn't the same everywhere though. How do other societies compare?

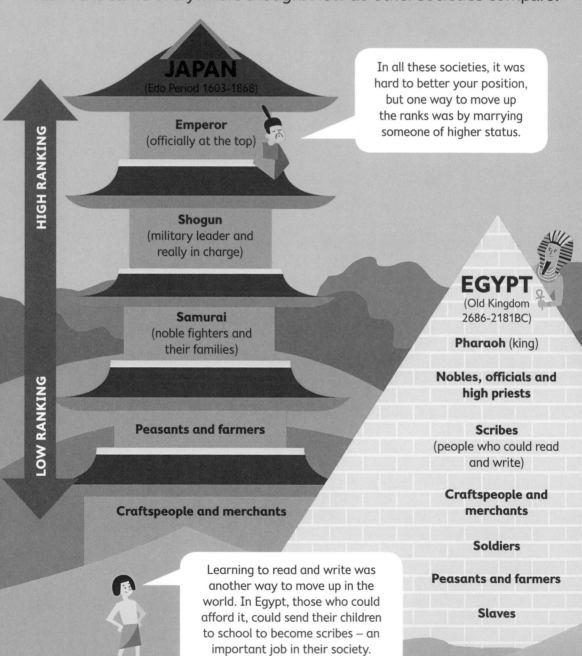

JAPAN
(Edo Period 1603–1868)

HIGH RANKING

LOW RANKING

Emperor
(officially at the top)

Shogun
(military leader and really in charge)

Samurai
(noble fighters and their families)

Peasants and farmers

Craftspeople and merchants

In all these societies, it was hard to better your position, but one way to move up the ranks was by marrying someone of higher status.

EGYPT
(Old Kingdom 2686–2181BC)

Pharaoh (king)

Nobles, officials and high priests

Scribes
(people who could read and write)

Craftspeople and merchants

Soldiers

Peasants and farmers

Slaves

Learning to read and write was another way to move up in the world. In Egypt, those who could afford it, could send their children to school to become scribes – an important job in their society.

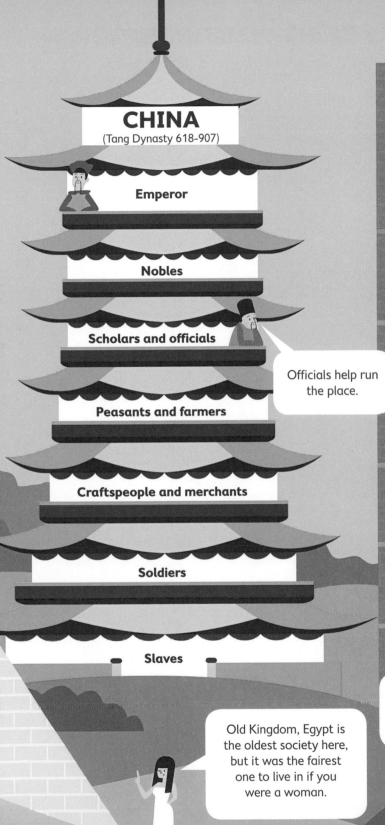

CHINA
(Tang Dynasty 618–907)

Emperor

Nobles

Scholars and officials

Peasants and farmers

Craftspeople and merchants

Soldiers

Slaves

Officials help run the place.

MEDIEVAL EUROPE
(1000–1500)

King

Nobles and high-ranking priests

Knights, lesser nobles and government officials

Craftspeople and merchants

Foot soldiers
(low-ranking men paid or forced to fight)

Peasants and farmers

Peasants, the biggest group in every society, farmed the land — but they didn't own any.

Old Kingdom, Egypt is the oldest society here, but it was the fairest one to live in if you were a woman.

Teaching children to read...

helped turn them into criminals – or did it?

By the late 19th century, school wasn't compulsory everywhere, but a lot of children in the UK and USA enjoyed reading. Most couldn't afford books, so publishers began selling cheap magazines known as **penny dreadfuls** or **dime novels**.

The magazines earned their names from their cheap cover price, a penny in Britain, or a dime in the USA.

Dramatic pictures on the covers often promised thrilling tales of criminals or scary monsters...

...stories that many adults began to believe were harmful to the children who read them.

SPRING HEELED JACK

Popular newspapers of the day – sold mainly to adults – ran headlines claiming these same stories were the cause of crime committed by the young.

British publisher Alfred Harmsworth made a small fortune creating and selling half-penny "story-papers" that he claimed were far less gruesome than the penny dreadfuls.

Harmsworth used his fortune to set up the *Daily Mail* and *Daily Mirror* newspapers, both of which linked reading of dreadfuls with child crime.

DAILY MAIL

YOUR CHILDREN COULD END UP IN COURT – BAN THIS SICK FILTH

By A. Harmsworth

It is an almost daily occurrence with magistrates to have before them boys who, having read a number of "dreadfuls", followed the examples set forth in such publications, robbed their employers, bought revolvers with the proceeds and finished by running away from home and installing themselves in the back streets as "highwaymen". This and many other evils the "penny dreadful" is responsible for. It makes thieves of the coming generation, and so helps fill our gaols.

No one has ever found hard evidence that reading the wrong sort of book makes a person more likely to commit a crime.

78 Shopkeepers not goldminers...
made the fastest millions in the Gold Rush.

In 1848, a mill owner found gold in a river in California, USA. The news soon spread to a nearby shopkeeper named Samuel Brannan, who told as many people as he could.

Within a year some 300,000 prospectors – gold hunters – arrived from all over the world, an event that came to be known as the **California Gold Rush**.

Before heading off into the hills where the gold was, they all stopped at stores to buy supplies. Brannan's was the best known.

SAM BRANNAN'S
OF SAN FRANSISCO

Lucky prospectors could expect to earn the equivalent of six years' wages for just six months of hard work.

By 1853, around
370 tons
of gold had been unearthed.

Brannan became a millionaire in 1849, without having to find and dig up any gold himself.

His home town, San Francisco, grew from **200** people to **36,000** in just five years.

after her death.

Inês de Castro was maid to the wife of Prince Peter of Portugal. She and Prince Peter fell in love, and, when Peter's wife died, he wanted to marry her. But Peter's father, King Alfonso IV, forbade the marriage and had her executed.

It is claimed that when Peter became king in 1357, he had Inês's body dug up and crowned queen, as a sign of his love and respect for her.

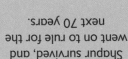

Shapur survived, and went on to rule for the next 70 years.

Of Shapur's three older brothers, one had been killed, one blinded and the third exiled.

was still in his mother's womb.

East and parts of Central Asia. But, legend has it, he was crowned while he became the next ruler of the **Sasanian Empire** – which covered the Middle After the death of his father, Hormzid II, in the year 390, Shah Shapur II

before his birth.

80 A baby became an emperor...

81 Muslim and Christian armies...
both made one Spanish warrior their hero.

A Spanish nobleman named Rodrigo Díaz de Vivar, known today as **El Cid** – Moorish for "Lord" – won battles for Christian kingdoms in the north of Spain, then fought for opposing Moorish kingdoms in the east.

In the 11th century, most of Spain was ruled by the **Moors** – Muslims from North Africa. But a group of squabbling Christian kingdoms held onto power in the north.

Christian kingdoms

Zaragoza

Valencia

Moorish kingdoms

Rodrigo Díaz won victories for Spanish King Sancho II against the Moors and against Sancho's brother, Alfonso.

When Alfonso became ruler after Sancho's death, he banished Rodrigo from the kingdom.

Rodrigo began fighting for the Moorish kingdom of Zaragoza. After many victories, the Moors named their hero Al Sidi or El Cid.

When new armies invaded from Africa, Alfonso persuaded El Cid to return to help him fight them.

El Cid conquered many Moorish cities for Alfonso, including Valencia, where El Cid brought Christians and Muslims to live and work together.

82 An assassin's umbrella...

killed a BBC journalist.

Georgi Markov, a journalist from Bulgaria, was assassinated by a poisoned pellet fired from an umbrella. The attack took place on Waterloo Bridge, London, in 1978.

Markov felt a sharp pain in his leg and noticed a man with an umbrella near him.

He died four days later. Doctors discovered a pellet containing a poison called **ricin** in his leg.

Markov had been critical of the Bulgarian government. His assassin was thought to be a spy, working for the Bulgarian secret service.

The assassination happened at the height of the **Cold War**, a long period of political tension and spying activity lasting from 1947 to 1991, between the **Western Bloc** and communist countries of the **Eastern Bloc**.

WESTERN BLOC
Most countries in western Europe and Scandinavia, as well as Greece, Turkey, Canada and the USA.

EASTERN BLOC
Bulgaria, Hungary, Poland, Romania, Czechoslovakia, East Germany and the Soviet Union – a group of 15 states including Russia.

The biggest ever bomb...

didn't kill anybody.

In 1961, Soviet soldiers and scientists in the Arctic detonated the most powerful bomb in human history: a nuclear bomb known as the **Tsar Bomba**. Luckily, it was just a test, and no one was hurt.

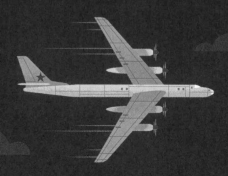

The bomb was dropped onto its target zone from a plane.

Before the test, the pilots were given just a 50% chance of surviving the blast – but they managed to land safely.

The explosion sent a shock wave through the Earth's crust that could be measured even after it had circled the globe **three times**.

The explosion was so powerful that in Norway, 900km (560 miles) away, **windows shattered**.

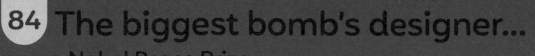

84 The biggest bomb's designer...

won a Nobel Peace Prize.

Andrei Sakharov was a Russian nuclear scientist who helped design the Tsar Bomba. He was horrified by the bomb's destructive power.

He went on to campaign for an end to nuclear testing and the arms race between eastern and western powers in the post-war years.

Sakharov won the Nobel Peace Prize in 1975.

What were the effects within the bomb's target zone?

The Tsar Bomba released

TEN TIMES

more energy than **ALL** the explosives used in the Second World War.

Within 100km (62 miles): **everything on fire**

Within 35km (22 miles): **total destruction**

85 A handshake in Europe...

sealed a scramble in Africa.

In the late 19th century, **90%** of Africa was under the control of a few European countries. At a conference in Berlin in 1884, European politicians agreed that Congo was the property of a Belgian company – and that other European companies could claim ownership of African regions, too.

After the conference, European leaders quickly set up official borders in "their" territories, sometimes simply by drawing lines across paper maps.

In Africa itself, many communities were divided, overnight, by new borders. The legacy of this is still causing political unrest today.

Ethiopia and Liberia remained independent – the rest of Africa was divided up.

Ethiopia

Liberia

European newspapers at the time described the process as **the Scramble for Africa**.

86 A secret underground railroad...
had neither trains, tracks nor tunnels.

From 1787 to 1860, many runaway slaves escaped the southern US states along a network of safehouses to northern states, or Canada, where they could live freely. These routes became known as the underground railroad.

Fugitives crossed fields, rivers and swamps in the dark. They hid in woods, barns or safe houses in the day.

One escaped slave named Harriet Tubman risked her life over and over again to guide more than 70 runaways to freedom.

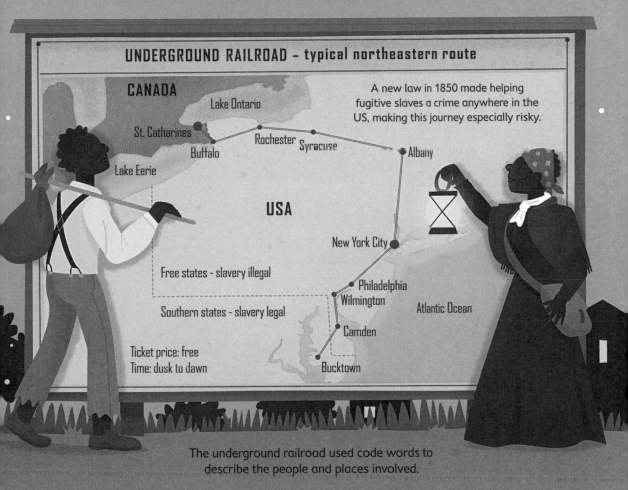

UNDERGROUND RAILROAD – typical northeastern route

CANADA

A new law in 1850 made helping fugitive slaves a crime anywhere in the US, making this journey especially risky.

Lake Ontario

St. Catharines

Rochester   Syracuse

Buffalo

Lake Eerie

Albany

USA

New York City

Free states - slavery illegal

Philadelphia
Wilmington

Atlantic Ocean

Southern states - slavery legal

Camden

Ticket price: free
Time: dusk to dawn

Bucktown

The underground railroad used code words to describe the people and places involved.

Station	**Station master**	**Conductor**	**Stockholder**
Safe house or barn, where escaped slaves could stay	Owner of safe house	Guide, who found a secure route between safe houses	Person who donated food, money or clothing

87 A six-year-old girl...

needed security guards to get to school every day.

In 1960, a change in the law in the US state of Louisiana allowed Black children to go to the same schools as white children for the first time – if they passed a test. The change in the law was a step forward for civil rights, but it still took time for people's attitudes to change.

Six-year-old Ruby Bridges was the only Black girl to join a school in her district of New Orleans.

Many families in the district were angry, and stood outside the school to protest...

...so armed marshals were sent to escort Ruby to the school, to make sure no one attacked her.

Day 1
After braving shouts and jeers from a mob of angry racists, Ruby found herself alone at school. The other children, and the staff, were sent home.

Day 2
A white teacher from Boston came to the school to teach Ruby. There were still no other children at the school.

Day 3
A tiny handful of white children came to the school, but were kept in a separate class. Ruby was taught in her own classroom, and even ate lunch on her own, for an entire school year.

Year 2
Aged seven, Ruby kept going to the same school, finally able to travel without her escorts. This time, one other Black child and a handful of white children joined her in her class.

By the time she left the school, aged 11, there were white and Black children in every class.

88 An emperor rewrote history...

by burning all the history books.

In 221BC, Emperor Qin Shi Huang brought peace to China after centuries of civil war. In one of his first acts as emperor, Qin Shi Huang ordered that all known history books should be burned. He made sure all new history books described him as a hero...

All over the world, conquering leaders have tried to erase their enemies' cultural history by destroying books, art and monuments.

When: 1193
Where: Nalanda, India
What: Turk general Bakhtiar Khilji destroyed much of the city, including its university – home to many thousands of Hindu and Buddhist texts.

When: 1427
Where: South America
What: Aztec ruler Itzcoatl ordered the destruction of all historical records from the peoples he conquered.

When: 1562
Where: Mexico
What: A Catholic bishop ordered all Maya records to be destroyed, to prevent any revival of their native religion.

When: 1814
Where: Washington D.C., USA
What: British troops burned down the Library of Congress, destroying around **6,000** volumes of American history, philosophy and literature.

When: 1939-44
Where: Warsaw, Poland
What: Nazi troops burned down many libraries, destroying around **16 million** volumes of literature.

89 A brief reign and a sticky end...

awaited most of the Byzantine emperors.

Politics in the Byzantine Empire (see opposite) tended to be chaotic and violent. Emperors reigned, on average, for just 11–12 years. They were often killed – or pushed into unpleasant retirement – by rivals, disloyal servants and impatient relatives. Here are the various ways, some overlapping, that most of the emperors ended their reigns.

Died while on the throne

Died of natural causes (illness or old age)

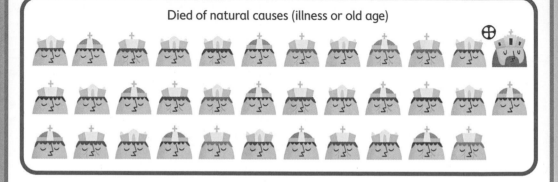

Died in an accident

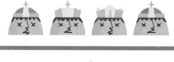

Murdered or executed

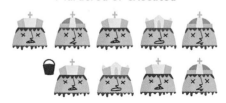

Died under suspicious circumstances

Mortally wounded in battle

Emperor Constans II was killed, while taking a bath, by a disgruntled servant wielding a heavy bucket.

The Byzantine Empire
Succeeding the Roman Empire, the Byzantine Empire held sway in the eastern Mediterranean from the 4th to the 15th century. Its capital city was Constantinople, now Istanbul.

Some emperors appear in this diagram more than once. **Emperor John V Palaiologos** appears three times. He was deposed once by his son and once by his grandson.

He managed both times to regain his throne. His third reign ended when he died of natural causes.

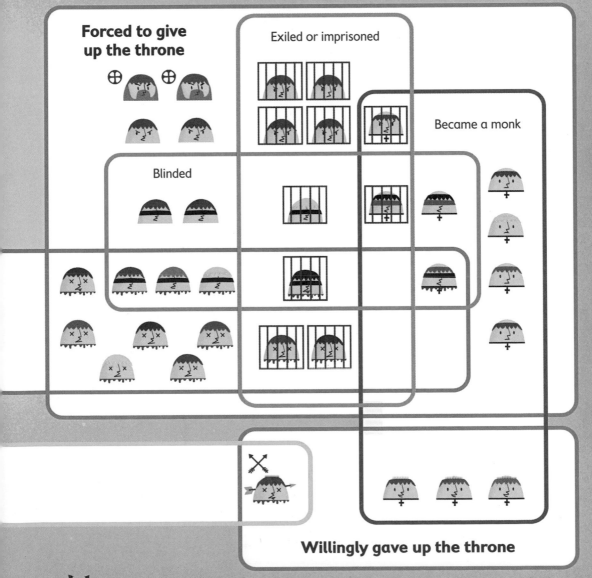

Forced to give up the throne

Exiled or imprisoned

Became a monk

Blinded

Willingly gave up the throne

Emperor Staurakios had the Byzantine Empire's shortest reign. He was gravely wounded in a battle just before being crowned emperor, and gave up the throne after a mere **69 days**. He died of his wound a few months later.

90 Women wore no underpants...

in medieval Europe.

In the Middle Ages, most people only had one set of clothes. They kept them clean by wearing linen underclothes, which were much easier to wash. Most women didn't wear underpants though...

There were no machines. All washing was done by hand with water from rivers and heated over fires.

Men wore "braies" – a kind of underpants, underneath a shirt.

Women wore a long shirt called a shift or smock, usually with nothing underneath.

91 For 13 years, Portugal's capital...

was in Brazil.

In 1807, the entire Portuguese royal court sailed from Lisbon, the capital of Portugal, to Rio de Janeiro in Brazil, a Portuguese colony at the time. They escaped days before the French army began an invasion of Lisbon.

More than 10,000 Portuguese nobles sailed in 36 ships, carrying all their gold, silver, furniture, paintings and state papers.

Although the French were fought off by 1811, the royal court only returned in 1821, to put down a rebellion.

By the 16th century, men were wearing knee or ankle length pants called drawers instead of braies.

Englishwomen started wearing underpants at the end of the 18th century – the last Europeans to do so.

Most European women started wearing stays or corsets to shape their bodies and lots of women started wearing drawers, too.

92 An outbreak of lice...
started a new fashion in Brazil.

On the voyage from Portugal to Brazil, a lice infestation forced the Portuguese princesses to shave their heads and throw their wigs overboard. They covered their heads in pork fat and antiseptic powder, and wrapped them in turbans.

When the princesses stepped off their ship wearing turbans, the women of Rio de Janeiro assumed it was the latest fashion in Europe, and started wearing turbans too.

Ooh – what stylish headdresses!

A family of bankers...

produced three popes, two queens and eight dukes.

In the 13th century, a small family from Florence, named Medici, set up a small business lending money. By 1397, the business had grown so large they set up one of the first banks in Europe. In time Cosimo the Elder took control of the city itself.

Duke

Pope

Queen

Giovanni di Bicci de' Medici
(born 1360)

I was so wealthy and powerful I set myself up as Gran Maestro of Florence.

Cosimo
(the Elder)

Piero I
(the Gouty)

Lorenzo I
(the Magnificent)

My great-grandfather started a small business. I turned it into an international bank.

As well as wielding political power, wealthy Medicis – especially Lorenzo I – funded many artists and scientists. They helped bring about a cultural movement known today as the **Italian Renaissance**.

Giovanni
– became
Pope Leo X

Lorenzo

Pier Francesco

Giovanni Popolani

Giovanni dalle bande nero

Giuliano

Giulio
– became
Pope Clement VII

Lucrezia

Francesca

Giuliano

Ippolito

Piero II
(the Unfortunate)

Lorenzo II

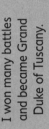

I won many battles and became Grand Duke of Tuscany.

Cosimo I

Alessandro
– became
Pope Leo XI

My father spent too much money, and I imposed too many taxes. Tuscany lost much of its power.

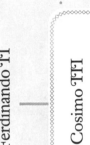

Ferdinando I

Cosimo II

Ferdinando II

Cosimo III

Gian Gastone
(the last Medici, died in 1737 with no children)

Alessandro
(First Duke of Florence)

Francesco I

Marie
– became Queen
regent of France

My husband, King Henry II, died young – I helped my sons, Francis II, Charles IX and Henry III, rule France for 30 years.

Catherine
– became Queen
consort of France

My husband, King Henry IV, died the day after I was crowned Queen of France. What a coincidence! I ruled the country until my son was old enough to take over as King Louis XIII.

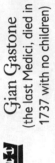

94 A night at the opera...

sparked a revolution.

In 1830, people living in Brussels, then part of the Kingdom of the Netherlands, were growing increasingly angry with their Dutch ruler, William I. An opera put on to mark his birthday inspired a major protest.

La Muette de Portici by Daniel Auber

In Act IV, two characters sing passionately of love for their country and hate for their foreign king.

With the song ringing in their ears, the crowd burst into the streets and stormed government buildings.

A month of fighting followed, until William gave in – and the Kingdom of Belgium was born.

95 Suleiman the Magnificent...

had more than 50 other titles.

Rulers are officially known by titles that list all their territories. The longest ever imperial title belonged to Suleiman the Magnificent, Sultan of the Ottoman Empire from 1520-1566:

His Imperial Majesty the Sultan Suleiman I, Sovereign of the Imperial House of Osman, Sultan of Sultans, Khan of Khans, Commander of the Faithful and Successor of the Prophet of the Lord of the Universe, Protector of the Holy Cities of Mecca, Medina and Jerusalem, Emperor of the Three Cities of Constantinople, Adrianople and Bursa, and of the Cities of Damascus and Cairo, of all Armenia, of the Magris, of Barka, of Kairuan, of Aleppo, of Arabic Iraq and of Ajim, of Basra, of El Hasa, of Dilen, of Raka, of Mosul, of Parthia, of Diyarbakir, of Cilicia, of the Vilayets of Erzurum, of Sivas, of Adana, of Karaman, of Van, of Barbary, of Abyssinia, of Tunisia, of Tripoli, of Damascus, of Cyprus, of Rhodes, of Candia, of the Vilayet of the Morea, of the Marmara Sea, the Black Sea and also its coasts, of Anatolia, of Rumelia, Baghdad, Kurdistan, Greece, Turkistan, Tatay, Circassia, of the two regions of Kabarda, of Georgia, of the plain of Kypshak, of the whole country of the Tarters, of Kefa and of all the surrounding countries, of Bosnia and its dependencies, of the City and Fort of Belgrade, of the Vilayet of Serbia, with all the castles, forts and cities, of all Albania, of all Iflak and Bogdania.

96 Infants were on the battlefront...
of the Mexican Revolution.

Throughout history, women have accompanied armies to war. During the **Mexican Revolution** (1910-1920), women, known as **soldaderas**, sometimes carried food to men at the battlefront, bringing young children with them.

Soldaderas cared for the wounded and brought food and coffee to men in the trenches.

Many soldaderas took part in the fighting too.

Women and children made up nearly a third of one army unit, led by **General Mercado**.

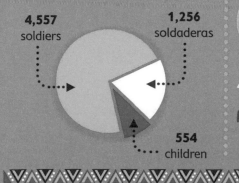

4,557 soldiers

1,256 soldaderas

554 children

Some women became commanding officers, known as **coronelas**, in charge of hundreds of men.

Capitana Clara Ramos led 70 men from the Mexican-US border into battle.

Petra Herrera joined the army disguised as a man. She was known for blowing up bridges and leading many dangerous missions.

97 Slaves became celebrities...

and helped abolish slavery.

In 1770s and 1780s, a slave and a former slave became famous as published authors. Their work gave the plight of slaves a human face and helped convince people that slavery should be abolished.

Phillis Wheatley, as she was named by her owners, was only eight years old when she was bought in 1761. Within a year she had learned to read and write.

Olaudah Equiano, a former slave, joined the anti-slavery movement in London in the 1780s.

By the time she was thirteen she was writing poetry. It made her a celebrity in New York and Boston, and later in London.

He published his autobiography in 1789, which became a UK bestseller.

It was published in German and Dutch, earning him international fame and fortune too.

Unlike Equiano, Wheatley was still a slave, so her owners had to approve of what she had written.

Reading Equiano or Wheatley showed Europeans they were wrong to think they were superior to those of African descent and that slavery was immoral. Slavery was eventually abolished in the UK in 1833, and in the US in 1865.

98 Rabbis, priests and imams...
relied on each other's work.

In the Middle Ages, Christian rulers in Europe fought the Muslims outside its borders and persecuted Jews within them. But rising above the violence, great thinkers from all three religions – Judaism, Christianity and Islam – exchanged knowledge and ideas freely.

One of them was the **Jewish Rabbi Moseh ben Maimon**, known as **Maimonides**. He lived in Spain under Muslim rule, then Egypt, where he was doctor to the Sultan. He spoke and wrote his most important work, *Guide for the Perplexed* (1190) in Arabic – the language of the Muslim holy texts.

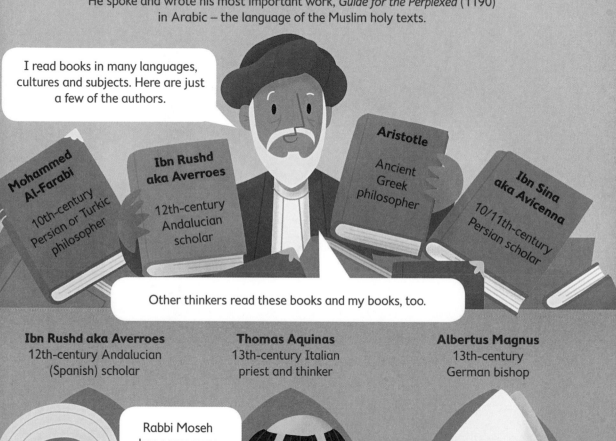

I read books in many languages, cultures and subjects. Here are just a few of the authors.

Mohammed Al-Farabi
10th-century Persian or Turkic philosopher

Ibn Rushd aka Averroes
12th-century Andalucian scholar

Aristotle
Ancient Greek philosopher

Ibn Sina aka Avicenna
10/11th-century Persian scholar

Other thinkers read these books and my books, too.

Ibn Rushd aka Averroes
12th-century Andalucian (Spanish) scholar

Thomas Aquinas
13th-century Italian priest and thinker

Albertus Magnus
13th-century German bishop

Rabbi Moseh has some very interesting thoughts on Aristotle.

I was born in Spain, at around the same time as Maimonides.

Guide for the Perplexed

99 A rescue mission for Napoleon...

might have succeeded with a submarine.

Napoleon Bonaparte was a brilliant general who led France to victory in wars of conquest throughout Europe, and became Emperor of France in 1804. After his final defeat at the battle of Waterloo in 1815, he was imprisoned on a remote South Atlantic island called St. Helena.

Napoleon may have been the most carefully guarded prisoner in history:

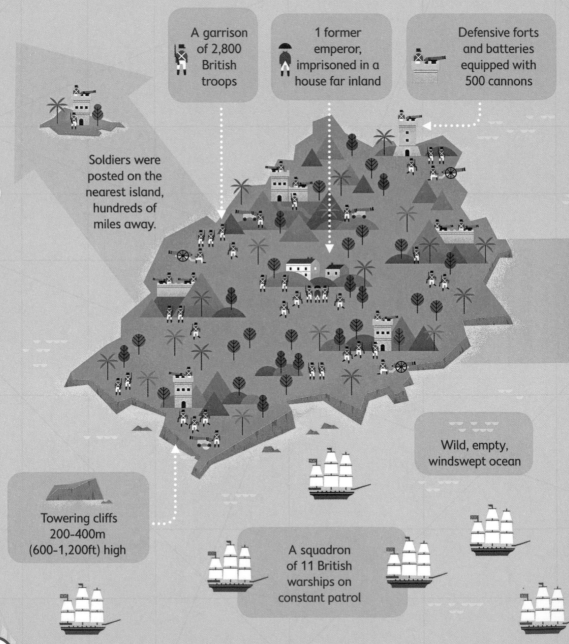

A garrison of 2,800 British troops

1 former emperor, imprisoned in a house far inland

Defensive forts and batteries equipped with 500 cannons

Soldiers were posted on the nearest island, hundreds of miles away.

Wild, empty, windswept ocean

Towering cliffs 200–400m (600–1,200ft) high

A squadron of 11 British warships on constant patrol

Why were these precautions necessary?

Napoleon still had many powerful supporters around the world – and he had already escaped from an island once before.

In fact, several plots *were* hatched to rescue Napoleon. Some were foiled; others were just getting underway...

...but, in 1821, before any rescue could be carried out, the former emperor died. The cause was probably stomach cancer.

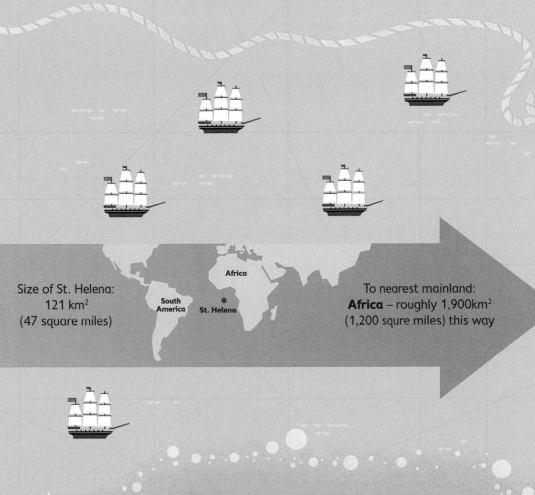

Size of St. Helena:
121 km²
(47 square miles)

Africa

South America

St. Helena

To nearest mainland:
Africa – roughly 1,900km²
(1,200 squre miles) this way

One daring rescue plan was to slip beneath the British ships in a primitive **submarine**, and lower the emperor down the cliffs on a rope. Submarines were still at an experimental stage in the 1820s – but some historians believe construction of a steam-powered rescue sub had begun.

100 The end of the world...

is always nigh.

Throughout history, people have often predicted that the world will come to an end, typically within their own lifetime. If you're reading this, none of these predictions has come true. But that hasn't stopped "experts" from warning people about the end of days, time and time again...

Around **2800BC**, text on an Assyrian tablet claimed that bribery, corruption and disobedient children were signs of the end of the world.

In **500AD**, three Christian scholars were the first to predict the Second Coming of Jesus Christ, an event that would – according to the Bible – herald the end of the world. Christians have re-predicted this event almost once every century.

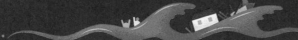

German astronomer Johannes Stöffler announced that a great flood would ravage Europe in 1524. Although it did rain on the exact day he predicted for the start of the flood, there was no damage.

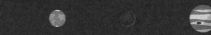

In the 1970s, two astronomers calculated that all the planets would align on the same side of the Sun in **1982** – an event they believed would trigger gravitational disaster on Earth.

01 02 03 04 05 06 07 08 09 10 11 12 13 14 15 16 17 18 19 20 21 22 23 24 25 26 27 28 29 30 31 32 33 34 35 36 37 38 39 40 41 42 43 44 45 46 47 48 49 50 51 52 53 54 55 56 5

THE END IS NIGH!

The final book in the Bible, known as the *Revelation to Saint John*, describes what will happen after the second coming of Christ. Four horsemen will spread war, famine, pestilence and death, bringing about the end of the world.

In fact, the planets align in this way once every few centuries — with no noticeable impact on the Earth.

January 1, 2000

In the 1990s, some IT experts warned that internal computer clocks, triggered to reset to "00" on midnight, **January 1, 2000**, would shut down all computers, causing global chaos. It didn't happen.

Mayan calendars, dating back over 5,000 years, used a system of marking days that was not endless. The "final day" happened to fall on **December 21, 2012**. Although it's unlikely the Maya believed the world would end on that date, some modern people did.

When did it happen?

These pages act as a timeline for major events or periods described in the book. Remember, c. stands for the Latin word *circa*, meaning "around" and it goes in front of dates of which historians are unsure. The numbers after each entry show which of the "100 things" describe each event or period.

c.3300–c.1300BC Indus Valley civilization, Pakistan and northwest India – **22**

c.2686–c.2181BC Old Kingdom of Egypt – **76**

c.1860–c.1814BC Reign of Pharaoh Amenemhat III in Egypt – **17**

c.1500BC Polynesian islanders began exploring and settling the South Pacific – **62**

c.1500-300BC Phoenician civilization – **47**

c.1478–c.1458BC Reign of Pharaoh Hatshepsut in Egypt – **67**

1100-1000BC *Epic of Gilgamesh* written down, oldest known epic poem – **69**

510BC Democracy began in Athens – **58**

c.500BC Birth of Mahavira – **21**

c.440BC Oldest known work of history, published by Herodotus in Greece – **2**

259-210BC Life of Qin Shi Huang, first Emperor of China – **54, 88**

218BC Hannibal of Carthage crossed the Alps to attack the Romans – **12**

c.6-4BC Likely birth of Jesus Christ – **1**

AD1 Original calculated date of the birth of Jesus Christ – **1**

70-80 Colosseum built in Rome – **75**

2nd century Cai Lun invented paper – **3**

117 The Roman Empire reached its largest extent, under Emperor Trajan – **46**

4th-15th centuries Byzantine Empire in eastern Europe and the Mediterranean – **89**

390 Shapur II crowned Shah of Sasanian Empire in Persia, ancient Iran – **80**

477-495 Reign of King Kashyapa I in Sri Lanka – **63**

6th century Secret of silk-making stolen from China and brought to Europe – **64**

541-546 Plague of Justinian – **65**

618-907 Tang Dynasty in China – **76**

632 Queen Seondeok of Silla united the kingdoms that would become Korea – **57**

780-1070 Age of Vikings – **14**

11th-15th centuries The Middle Ages or Medieval period in Europe – **5, 6, 50, 76, 90**

1040-1099 Life of El Cid – **81**

1122-1204 Life of Eleanor of Aquitaine – **15**

1135-1204 Life of Maimonides – **98**

1312-1337 Reign of Musa I in Mali – **48**

1346-1353 Black Death – **34, 65**

1357 Inês de Castro crowned Queen of Portugal – **79**

1368 Ming Dynasty founded in China – **8**

1374 "Choreomania" broke out in western Europe – **6**

14th-16th centuries Italian Renaissance – **93**

1434-1737 The Medici family held power in Florence, northern Italy – **93**

1520-1566 Reign of Suleiman the Magnificent over the Ottoman Empire – **95**

1532 Francisco Pizarro defeated Atahualpa, last ruler of Inca Empire in Peru – **37**

1582 Pope Gregory XIII introduced the Gregorian calendar – **10**

1593 Irish pirate Gráinne Ní Mháille met Elizabeth I, Queen of England – **44**

15th-19th centuries Slave trade between western Africa and the Americas – **61**

c.1600-1800 Oyo Empire in Nigeria – **57**

1603-1868 Edo Period in Japan – **53, 76**

1636-1637 "Tulip mania" resulted in price surge and crash in the Netherlands – **38**

1752 Britain switched from the Julian to the Gregorian calendar – **10, 11**

1753-1784 Life of poet Phillis Wheatley – **97**

18th century Settlers in North America developed new felling axes – **4**

c.1745-1797 Life of Olaudah Equiano, writer and anti-slavery campaigner – **97**

19th century World population reached one billion, and began rising rapidly – **66**

1805 British Vice Admiral Horatio Nelson killed during the Battle of Trafalgar – **68**

1808-1821 Portuguese capital moved from Lisbon to Rio de Janeiro, Brazil – **91**

1811 Luddite uprising began in Britain – **41**

1815 French Emperor Napoleon was defeated and exiled to St. Helena – **99**

1830 Belgium won independence from the Kingdom of the Netherlands – **94**

1840s-1870s British tax inspectors grew "the Great Hedge" of India – **18**

1844 The first official international sports match was held in New York – **30**

1845 John Franklin led an ill-fated expedition to find the Northwest Passage – **20**

1848-1855 "Gold rush" in California, US – **78**

c.1850 Steam trains overtook horses as the fastest way to travel – **35**

1850s-1860s The "underground railroad" was at its peak in the eastern US – **86**

1860s "Guanomania" sparked conflict in South America – **55**

1861-1865 Civil War in the US – **39, 40**

1880s Steam ships overtook sail ships as the fastest way to cross the ocean – **35**

1884 The Berlin Conference started a European "scramble for Africa" – **85**

1888 Slavery made illegal in Brazil – **61**

1889 First voyage around the world using public transportation – **36**

1893 New Zealand became the first country to let women vote in elections – **59**

1910-1920 Mexican Revolution – **96**

1914-1918 First World War – **9, 13, 42, 71**

1917 Russian Revolution – **42, 52**

1919 Planes overtook ships as the fastest way to cross the Atlantic Ocean – **35**

1924 Death of Lenin – **43**

1930 "Salt March" in India – **52**

1939-1945 Second World War – **22, 72**

1945 Two nuclear bombs hit Japan – **19**

1947-1991 Cold War – **82**

1950s-1960s Civil Rights movement in America – **52, 87**

1961 Russian hydrogen bomb *Tsar Bomba* detonated in the Arctic Ocean – **83**

1967 Six Day War between Israel and nearby Arab states, Egypt, Jordan and Syria – **49**

1978 Bulgarian Georgi Markov assassinated in London – **82**

1989 Human chain of protest in Estonia, Latvia and Lithuania – **73**

2002 President Chavez arrested, and immediately released in Venezuela – **52**

2003 Worldwide anti-war protests – **52**

2012 The Maya calendar reached its final day, but the world did not end – **100**

2015 Women gained the right to vote in elections in Saudi Arabia – **59**

Where did it happen?

The numbers on this map of the world show you where some of the "100 things" in this book happened.

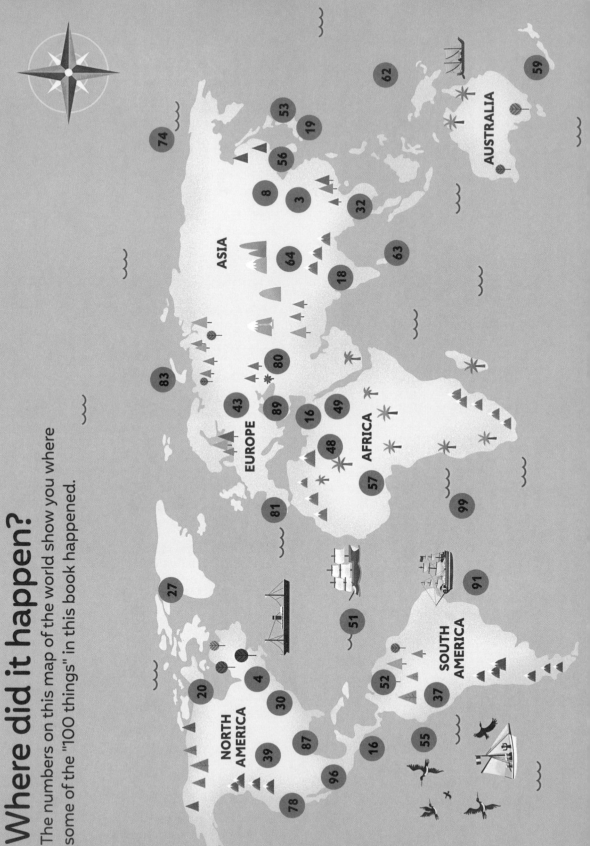

Key:

3 Paper invented by Chinese official Cai Lun.

4 New axes made by settlers in North America.

8 Ming dynasty founded; Great Wall completed.

16 Pyramids built in Maya Empire and Ancient Egypt.

18 Great Hedge of India grown by British officials.

19 Atomic bombs destroyed Hiroshima and Nagasaki.

20 North-West Passage mapped.

27 Meteorite used to make tools in Greenland.

30 First international sporting event held in Manhattan.

32 Khmer Empire collapsed in Cambodia.

37 Incas conquered by the Spanish.

39 Up to 800,000 soldiers died in American Civil War.

43 Lenin's body displayed in Moscow.

48 Economic meltdown in North Africa.

49 Merchant ships stuck for eight years in Suez Canal.

51 Transatlantic slave trade.

52 Protestors marched on Caracas, Venezuela.

53 Samurai warriors in Japan.

55 War fought in the Chincha Islands.

56 Temple built as to-do list by Korean queen.

57 Alaafin executed in Oyo Empire, Nigeria.

59 Women first allowed to vote in New Zealand.

62 Polynesian explorers set sail in canoes full of plants.

63 Palace fortress built by Sri-Lankan king.

64 Secret of silk stolen by monks from China.

74 Mammoths still alive on Wrangel Island in 2560BC.

78 Gold Rush in California.

80 Sasanian emperor crowned in mother's womb.

81 El Cid made a hero in Moorish Spain.

83 Tsar Bomba dropped on Soviet testing site.

87 Six-year-old girl taken to school by armed marshals in Louisiana.

89 Byzantine emperors murdered and deposed.

91 Portuguese royalty sailed to Rio de Janeiro

96 Women joined army in Mexican Revolution.

99 Napoleon exiled to St. Helena.

Turn the page for a map showing where things happened in Europe.

Where in Europe?

The numbers on this map of Europe show you where some of the "100 things" in this book happened.

Key:

6 Choreomania in Aachen

9 Cher Ami saved 200 men in Northern France.

12 Hannibal crossed the Alps.

13 Ships painted with dazzle camouflage fought in the First World War.

14 Vikings skied in Scandinavia.

15 Eleanor of Aquitaine

23 Coloman the Bookish ruled Hungary.

38 Tulip mania in the United Provinces

41 Weavers smashed their looms in England.

44 Gráinne Ní Mháille met Queen Elizabeth I in London.

46 Gladiators fought in the Colosseum at Rome.

58 Democracy was born in Athens.

73 A human chain crossed Estonia, Latvia and Lithuania.

74 Central stones erected at Stonehenge in 2560BC.

79 Inês de Castro crowned in Portugal.

85 Africa divided up by European leaders in Berlin.

93 The Medicis ruled Florence.

98 Birthplace of Maimonides

Index

Usborne Quicklinks

For links to websites where you can discover more surprising history facts with video clips, quizzes and activities, go to the Usborne Quicklinks website at **usborne.com/Quicklinks** and enter the keywords: **things to know about history**.

Here are some of the things you can do at the websites we recommend:

• translate your name into Egyptian hieroglyphs
• examine artifacts in museums around the world from eras spanning over 10,000 years of history
• test your knowledge of US presidents
• discover what happened on this day in history

Making a book...

involves several different jobs.

Research and writing:

Laura Cowan, Alex Frith, Minna Lacey and Jerome Martin

Layout and design:

Freya Harrison, Lenka Hrehova and Amy Manning

Illustration:

Federico Mariani and Parko Polo

additional illustration by Marc-Etienne Peintre

Series editor:
Ruth Brocklehurst

Series designer:
Stephen Moncrieff

History consultant:
Dr. Anne Millard